ICELAND

ICELAND

Born of lava chiseled by ice

ARNOLD ZAGERIS

Fitzhenry & Whiteside

Fitzhenry & Whiteside Limited acknowledges with thanks the Canada Council for the Arts and the Ontario Arts Council
for their support of our publishing program.
We acknowledge the financial support of the Government of Canada through the Canada Book Fund (CBF) for our publishing activities.

Library and Archives Canada Cataloguing in Publication
Title: Iceland : born of lava chiseled by ice / Arnold Zageris.
Names: Zageris, Arnold, 1948- author, photographer.
Identifiers: Canadiana 20200311395 | ISBN 9781554554775 (hardcover)
Subjects: LCSH: Zageris, Arnold, 1948—Travel—Iceland. | LCSH: Iceland—Description and travel. |
LCSH: Iceland—Pictorial works.
Classification: LCC DL315 . Z34 2020 | DDC 914.91204/6—dc23

Publisher Cataloging-in-Publication Data (U.S.)
Names: Zageris, Arnold, 1948-, author, photographer.
Title: Iceland : Born of Lava, Chiseled by Ice / Arnold Zageris.
Description: Markham, Ontario : Fitzhenry and Whiteside, 2021. | Summary: "Photographic celebration of Iceland"-- Provided by publisher.
Identifiers: ISBN 978-1-55455-477-5 (hardcover)
Subjects: LCSH: Iceland – Description and travel. | Iceland – Pictorial works. | BISAC: TRAVEL / Europe / Iceland & Greenland.
Classification: LCC DL315Z344 | DDC 914.912 – dc23

Text and cover design by Kerry Designs
Printed in Hong Kong by Sheck Wah Tong Printing

For Joan, my one and only.

After about a three-hour hike wandering over what seemed like a lifeless moon, I came across some familiar life forms: a few blades of grass. Though they were somewhat wind-beaten and dry they still managed to make their place in such an unforgiving landscape. Sunburned and thirsty I sat down and admired their tenacity and resilience.

ICELAND

Introduction

It was while we were navigating the northern coast of Labrador preparing for another summer's photography session that Tom Goodwin, the owner of our vessel, mentioned that we should keep a sharp lookout for a replica of a Viking ship. This surprised me. I knew nothing of this expedition and was told that weeks ago, on June 28th, 1998, a craft, christened The *Snorri*, left Nuuk, Greenland and had now reached the Labrador coast and was likely in our vicinity. Knowing this the three of us were eager to search the horizon thinking that just maybe we might be lucky to be the first to welcome them.

They were a crew of eight trying to replicate the Viking explorer, Leif Erikson's, voyage to the new world. It was a brave and audacious attempt to cross 1,800 miles of ocean in an exposed and primitive craft. All day we kept a sharp and steady lookout. Unfortunately, we never saw them but later found out that they were successful and had landed at the same spot where the Vikings established their first settlement in America. This knarr, or wooden merchant ship, was the focus of our attention and we all excitedly shared our thoughts about what the feelings were for these fearless sailors who left their homes a thousand years ago heading into an unknown. We imagined families parting, each side aware of the risks involved, fearing that it may be forever. All hoped that those leaving their familiar beaches, about to plunge into a cold and unknown sea, would eventually be delivered safely by favourable winds onto some friendly shore. However, we also realized that these men were more seaworthy than we think, having already explored and sacked England, the western coast of Europe and parts of the Mediterranean. With these new thoughts of Iceland strongly fixed in my mind I decided I would now focus on the island that was the stepping stone between the Scandinavian countries and Greenland. This idea persisted and its appeal took root. Here was a country that had an attractive geography and a hardened history. It was a land of fire and ice and had once been home to the notoriously feared Norsemen. With such a remarkable past and an active landscape that was being torn apart by the continental drift, spawning unpredictable volcanoes, melting massive glaciers and collapsing them into the sea, I knew it was here that I would find something to photograph.

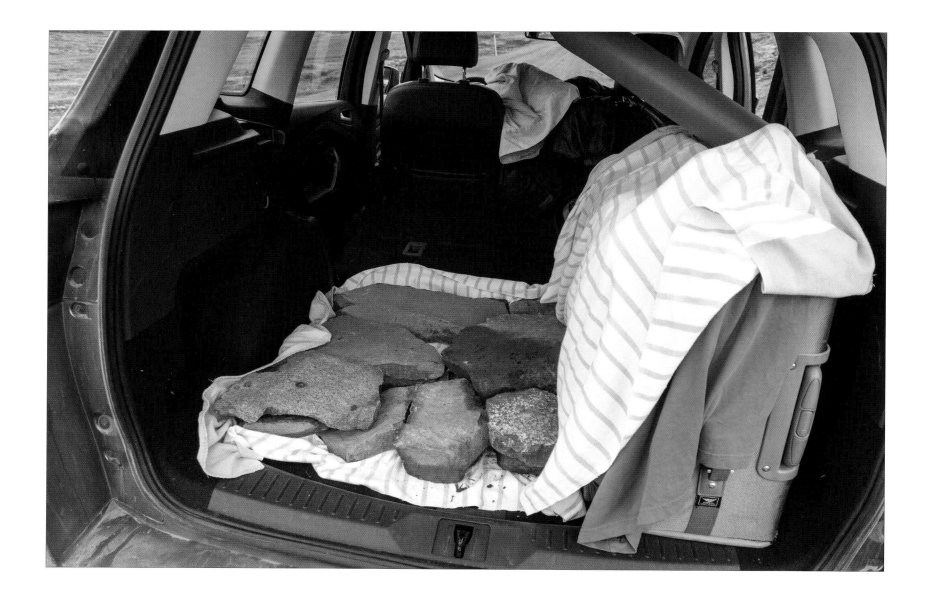

Step 1

Getting to Iceland could not be any easier. I leave Toronto in the evening and arrive at Keflavik airport in the morning, clear a speedy customs check, and pick up my prearranged leased vehicle just outside the terminal. I left home only 12 hours ago and now a one-minute drive already puts me in a lava field ready to be explored. Since my single purpose in being here is photography, I want to be in the outdoors where my subjects are, and be there when the light is right, so I sleep in the car to avoid commuting to time-consuming hotels. When you are deep inland and hours away from any other accommodation the car and tenting are the only options. The seats of this leased car do not fold down in a manner conducive to sleeping in a horizontal position, so a few adjustments are required. The ledge and slope were too pronounced so a few flat, hard-found stones in a round rock country, solved the problem. Here my flannel sheet kept the car clean and protected my mattress and sleeping bag. It has primitive look but after 18-hour days it feels just fine and when the sun comes up at 3:00 a.m. you are already where you want to be.

Step 2 Flannel cover folded over rocks   **Step 3** Self inflating air mattress.   **Step 4** Down sleeping bag

Step 5 Economical sleeping accommodations of a previous year

Travel is an English word that stems from the French word *travail* which means work, and all travelers know how difficult and energy draining this can be. Photographers, especially, who haul and hump all their precious gear into the most remote places, can suffer the challenges of their trade if they do not plan well. Many years of wilderness travel has taught me to whittle down my camera equipment to one or two digital cameras, a 24mm to 70mm zoom lens, a 70mm to 200mm zoom lens, extra memory cards, lens cleaning kit plus an indispensable tripod. My camera is an excuse to travel.

When I travel my prime objective is usually photography. I have been doing this for over 30 years, first concentrating on the area around my home and later journeying further to more remote areas such as Iceland, Labrador and Antarctica. In my earlier years I began by shooting slide film using a 35 mm camera, but then, at a photography workshop with Eliot Porter, he suggested I purchase a 4x5-inch large-format field camera. I followed his advice and it completely changed how I worked and radically transformed my approach to the photographic process. Now, with larger colour transparencies I was able to record the landscape in finer detail.

With the considerable expense of sheet film and film development I had to be more critical in my evaluation and number of exposures. The reward of each successful image was, however, substantial, and it had enough information to make larger prints that were favoured by museums and galleries.

However, after 9/11 the security issues and rigorous inspection of airplane carry-ons became an issue that was increasingly hard to deal with. Not only was everything X-rayed repeatedly, turning the film into a mikly haze, but when confronted by uniformed inspectors on the other side of the counter insisting on opening and exposing my film, it all became impossible. These triple-lid boxes were not familiar to some inspectors, nor were the metal casings of 35-mm film, and no amount of explaining would impress on them the damage they would do. Now that the high probability of having hard-earned photographs over-X-rayed or exposed to light during inspection was a guarantee, it quickly put an end to my travels with the view camera. Fortunately, and just in time, the digital age developed large enough camera sensors to allow large-image printing and, more importantly, the memory cards were not affected by X-rays. Additionally, there was no cost in taking as many pictures as needed. I welcomed the digital age.

ICELAND

Travelling by car through a new countryside searching for areas that might be of interest, I very often stop at random to take an easy walk without a camera to try and be in the moment. Sitting behind the wheel of a car for a good while can become desensitizing. Even through a clean windshield or an open window things cannot be truly appreciated and just pass too quickly, like objects flowing by on a continuously moving conveyor belt. You might appreciate the sudden appearance of a panoramic and compelling vista but the smaller features are unseen and totally lost. There is no time to examine and build up an emotional response to what you are travelling through. Also lost is the opportunity to feel the varying terrain through your shoes and to hear its crunching sound or to feel how the wind touches you differently when not being created by a moving car. The air gives up its smell and becomes part of what you are looking at. This arbitrary wandering, experiencing the landscape as a whole, gives me the strong feeling of really being there and a better understanding of the land that I have come to explore.

After five visits and travelling a few thousand kilometres on rough terrain I am rewarded with my first and only flat tire. Even though you fully expect this to happen, you are somewhat annoyed when it does. Especially in the rain.

ICELAND

Some individuals are a bit hesitant to enter a public or private gallery on the grounds that they do not feel competent or educated enough to judge or speak about a work of art. Afraid of possible embarrassment, they avoid the opportunity and unnecessarily miss out on a potentially stimulating and pleasurable experience. Having to make confident and assured judgments about my own work I use a four-step process that makes it easy to come to a positive or negative opinion that can be answered with the following questions.

> #1 What is it?
> #2 What is it about?
> #3 Is it any good?
> #4 Why or why not?

Let's do a quick look at this image for example.

Question #1 What is it?

The title tells you a little bit of what it is, but you also see some grey material spread over the lava that may be something like dried-up moss, and also there seems to be some new green growth as well. There are a couple of distinct ridges in the centre and a few hills further into the image. Then there is also something that looks like smoke.

Question #2 What is it about ?

Since it is about lava it must have something to do with a volcano and the new and the surrounding old plant growth shows that some time has passed, and it is now cooling down enough to support life. The smoke shows that this part is still active and very hot. The two long prominent ridges must be part of the tunnel that over time collapsed, leaving some of the tunnel wall intact and the centre of the tube lower than the surrounding lava flow.

Question#3 Its it any good?

Yes I think so.

Question #4 Why?

The picture is leaden and a bit sinister giving it a foreboding mood reminding me of the dark unfamiliar thing a volcano can be. The two colours of moss give me an indication that quite some time has passed since this spot was cool enough to support life. The collapsed lava tube helps me imagine what it was like when the hot liquid rock flowed easily through a guiding tunnel. The remaining twin lines in the centre help to make sure the eyes are led to the rising fumes coming from the vents. All the elements in this image tell a story that is still ongoing. The more I look at it the more I see and understand why or why not I am drawn to this image.

Remember that even though you find an image unappealing it could still be well-executed, possibly meaning its purpose was to repel. Not being attractive might make it effective in its message, so still warranting a "yes" answer.

Collapsed lava tube

I stood at the top of this hill and enjoyed the wide swing of the road and how it looked out of place in the vastness of the empty landscape. My camera and tripod were all set up and I was deciding on how much of the sky should be included and if I needed more foreground to make an engaging image. For a while I was composing and recomposing the picture, so much so that I soon realized I was forcing this image. I was trying to justify the image by observing how the curve of the road mimicked the area on the bottom right, and how the horizon somewhat mirrored the brooding sky. I took the picture anyway with the knowledge that it lacked something and that eventually I would delete it. Serendipitously, seconds later, with all my gear still in place, a speeding car raced into the picture bringing action and life into the image. I waited for the car to raise enough dust, still be in a desired spot, and emphatically pressed the shutter. Nothing was forced now. This picture easily made itself.

We all respond to beauty. We actively seek it out. I once heard a man say. "How can you not stop and look at a rainbow?" However, all beauty is not in bright and glowing colours. Sometimes beauty is quite monochromatic, subtle and subdued. Even the moon in its colourless form of black and grey was described by an astronaut as "a terrible beauty". I think there also is a beauty inspired purely by of awe and wonder. In this image I am feeling the clinging steam and smelling sulphur fumes still rising from a dormant volcano. It is evening and becoming gloomy with an "I shouldn't be here feeling". Beneath the blanketing haze are hidden colours of cooling rock, red and black. Muted coloured moss clings tentatively to a warming ash. In places where the earth is cracked with deep fissures a groaning can be heard; a rumbling from an unseeable abyss. It is unsettling and primordial. A terrible beauty.

Landscape photography is all about packaging your total emotional response into a frame that reflects what you felt at the moment. The only sense that you have to work with is the visual. Drop the sounds you heard or the wind you felt, drop the smell and taste, and just deal with making a convincing image composed of subject matter, composition, and all the qualities of light: colour, contrast, tone, brightness, shadows and highlights.

It was a late evening hike, but in these latitudes the summer sun sets reluctantly so I still wandered around the hills at a time where, in the lower latitudes, it would have been completely dark. All evening the scenery was continually filled with a varying light portraying a variety of compelling moods. Every passing minute the landscape was transformed, tempting me many times to set up my camera and capture it. However, at the end of this long day and maybe being more tired and more reluctant to set up my equipment, I let a few images go by that I then thought were just on the cusp of making the grade. But when the sky took this dramatic sombre turn my choice was made and I had found the drama that I was hoping for. Instead of focusing on the bright snow with streaks of black ash flowing down the hillside, I now focused my attention on the three brightening clouds that minutes before were dark and unnoticed. Now they were brighter than the snow, and had more presence. I lowered the horizon line and in a larger space and nearly mid frame they became the dominant feature, helping to emphasize a sullen landscape.

Flowing water has a hypnotic effect on everyone. It is an attractive force that must go deep inside our genetic makeup. Coming from an area where a waterfall or a rapidly moving stream is a rarity, I am particularly taken by the innumerable water chutes, cascades and rivers of Iceland. I am not necessarily speaking about the massive iconic ones that have captured the attention of the multitudes of visitors that yearly inundate these water-filled canyons, but those that are more insignificant, the ones most likely missed, which draw no particular mention in any guide book. I enjoy discovering and exploring these simply because they have so much more character than just being riveting volumes of water. The smaller minor ones are easily crossed and approachable from both sides making the compositional aspects more varied and challenging. A small alteration in position can make a major change in your image. On the downside though, the photographic options are sometimes so numerous and overwhelming that you might be inclined to work too quickly and come away with nothing. The only solution is to get away and return with a fresh and more settled and contemplative approach. These two different streams were taken two years apart after I first discovered them.

This image is a close up view of the larger waterfall in the next picture. It is not what one would call a minimalistic picture but it does come close. In a minimalistic image the subject is very evident and there is no hesitation on the part of the viewer as to what the picture is about. Here, however, it is still a tossup as to whether it is the cascading water, the single rock in the centre, or the also seemingly cascading rock and moss on the right.

It was suggested by a viewer that the single rock disrupts the picture and should be cloned out thereby giving full attention to the water. I considered this possible option but it was this rock that attracted my attention in the first place so I decided to leave it as it was. It is a strong focal point grounding the image and its darkness makes the water gleam brighter. Place a finger over the rock and decide what you would do.

If one studies this image long enough you will get the impression that all is flowing towards you. The downward flowing basalt columns hanging in the cliff face eventually break off and the waterfall also drops to the river bed below. The scale of the tumbled rocks becomes larger as they roll towards you and the blurred stream rushes past. A miniature waterfall on the left drops at its own speed. Rocks or water all must eventually flow to the sea.

Even though this moss took hundreds of years to establish itself, it takes but little time to give way and submit to gravity's will. Here you can see the downward path through the clinging moss that the water rivulets have taken. This is where the weakening and fracturing takes effect. On the left side a section of the hill has already slipped away and in the middle another crack has widened, weakening this tenuous slope. Over time all hills crumble, level out, and disappear.

This image does not have any grand features like big trees, imposing mountains or a dominating sky. It is a busy picture, but everything is interesting and compelling. The bright green moss, the red scattered leaves, and the yellow bush in the foreground immediately capture your attention. They glow with an even light, revealing all their intimate detail. Drifting deeper into the image the middle ground of a golden-brown forest leads us to a subdued horizon of dreary cloud-covered mountains. It is a complex picture with many elements that combine to entertain the eye with its depth, vivid and subtle colours, detail, and drama.

Few places in Iceland offer settings where there are trees. These dwarf white birch are in a protected valley sheltered from most of nature's harshest elements yet they still show signs of stress, bending to the effects of wind and ice.

I do not review my images immediately when I get home from a major trip but wait for about three weeks to allow those memorable moments to fade. Later, when I do begin to review my images, it feels like I am now looking at them for the first time but with a fresher and more critical eye. I could now judge them on their own merit and not be influenced by my surroundings and the thrill of being there. The images become objectified and I now see them more as another viewer would.

I think this picture of Iceland shows how empty and gloomy parts of Iceland can be. When travelling mile after mile in a landscape filled just with volcanic cinders and ash you get a very good sense of what it might feel like to be on the moon or some other unworldly planet with a similar atmosphere. It is all these unfamiliar sensations that make Iceland so exciting. I hiked many kilometres through lonely terrain like this and always felt some sort of relief when I got back and into the car. It became my safety capsule. It was dry and warm, had food, and a place where I could sleep safely tucked away from the elements such as the strong winds carrying stinging bits of ash that could scour the paint off a vehicle. In Keflavik, where I rented my car, I saw someone come back from a trip inland with half the car sandblasted. It was dark blue on one side and a baby blue on the other with hints of undercoating showing through. There is optional insurance for that too.

In late autumn these smooth rolling hills are still marked with last winter's snow. In summer these remnant patches of melting snow supply a consistent amount of water and the wind-borne ash provides fresh nutrients to the greener pastures below. Here the sun breaks through a cloudy sky, bathing the brown carpet of moss in a warmth that may be the last before the dark and cold arctic nights set in. The two flashes of white in the upper right-hand corner are newly opened crevasses indicating fresh activity in this steep collapsing snowfield.

ICELAND

An overcast day hangs over this extensive lava field cushioned by a soft soothing yellow moss. A shallow channel on the left leads into damp greener ditches spreading through the landscape. Suitable to this terrain, moss does not need any root system to absorb water, so living on impenetrable rock is not an issue as long as there is enough warmth sunshine and moisture.

In some lava fields the moss is stressed and not so well established.

Sometimes, as expected, the weather in Iceland can turn for the worse and can stay so for days. It does no good to step out of the car and head into an all-day rain. Living in a car makes it doubly difficult when all your gear and clothes are wet, and drying becomes another obstacle. The only option is to plan on where to go when the weather does improve and slowly drive that way or if the place looks promising just stay put and wait. The day then becomes something more like window shopping from a car. This image of a road that sweeps in a long elegant line bending to the lonely landscape is a good example of an opportunistic moment for photography. It also demonstrates how time consuming and difficult it can be to make an image that says more than "I took a picture and this is what it looked like."

This image has become a favourite of mine and has withstood the test of time. Often I become attached to some image for a short time and then let another take over. But this one is different. Not because it is better, but it has elements in it that please me visually and emotionally. I particularly like the bright reflective asphalt and the vivid road markers that swing across the whole landscape, drawing the eye into a hazy horizon dominated by three successively smaller hills. Far away and mysterious, they beckon and entice one to continue. My eye is constantly led to the little stretch of road that can be seen on the extreme right between the two hills. It leaves me wondering.

Initially I planned to wander slowly into these soft and easy flowing foothills looking for an opportunistic image, but after a half hour walk, the landscape had not changed and I realized it would take another three-quarters of an hour. With a return trip also to consider, my enthusiasm waned. Not to feel defeated I finally settled on a zoomed-in panorama.

Penetrating light

Trying to pre-visualize an image can often be very frustrating and time-consuming. Initially I was concentrating on the fog drifting past the mountain when a flock of sheep entered the scene. I watched them coming up from over the gravel bar, moving independently in all directions and then again disappearing. I was hoping they would come up towards me into full view so they would be reflected in the pond. However, when they did, they were all over the place and never formed an attractive grouping. It was a waiting game. My tripod was all set up and my camera pre-focused. When they finally did assemble they were too far to the right and I would lose the mountain as a backdrop. Suddenly they turned my way and with their reflections in tow, bunched up, waited for a straggler, looked at me, and gave me the image I was hoping for.

A delicate flower, the moss campion or cushion pink, dots the moist areas across the arctic tundra. I was told by a local farmer that some Icelandic people boiled and ate it, although he had yet to try it.

Beside the sea on a cool and peaceful day a solitary sheep feeds on a well-maintained farm. Our impression of farming and agriculture in Iceland is often misleading. We think it is a country of fire and ice and the weather is too cold and not conducive to such activities. However, the average winter temperature here is warmer than New York's. Iceland is known for its lush and nutritious grass. Long summer days of constant light promote strong growth in a rich soil and a temperate climate hinders the pest population. This also reduces drastically the need for harmful pesticides and promotes a healthy livestock.

Packaged hay

Iceland is an island nation like no other. Ten kilometres earlier I had been travelling through an unfriendly landscape surrounded by the darkest pillars of lava, and now unexpectedly I was driving above this sunlit golden pasture. The hills in the distance are still covered in fog, sheep graze in the greener fields while herds of horses move about freely reminding me of the wild horses of Sable Island off Nova Scotia.

Attentive to the photographer these sheep are about to settle into a pit in the hillside. Many times I have walked down a sloping field to be surprised by the sudden appearance of a couple of sheep seemingly coming out of the ground. Without any artificial shelter these self-made dugouts provide protection from Iceland's frequent wind and rain.

This image has a very special mood and quality. At the end of a long Icelandic day the warm glow of a setting sun reflects brightly off the backs of horses and sheep. All are heading home on this last day of a summer roundup. I can only imagine this man's satisfaction as he casually guides his flock, urging them down from the highland pastures into the valley below. The end of a long day and the end of a season.

The Icelandic horse has been a resident of Iceland since the days when the Norse settled here in the Ninth Century. Much beloved by locals and foreigners alike, it is a hardy species, mostly disease-free and capable of withstanding the Arctic's harsh climate. Affable by nature, they are easily trained for dressage and used for sheep roundup in the fall. To maintain the breed's distinct genetic pool Icelandic law prohibits any importation of horses, nor are they allowed to return once they have left the country.

I was impressed by how much the children, who accompanied the fall roundup, were eager to interact with all the animals in a warm and caring way. And it seemed the animals knew it too. However, as much as I enjoyed this interaction, as a photographer, I was particularly pleased with the children's outfits that nearly made the perfect colour wheel of magenta, yellow and cyan, red and green and blue.

When I took this picture my intention was to capture the tranquil demeanour of this gentle horse as it turned to face me. It was a strange juxtaposition with the calmness of the unconcerned horses on one side of the fence and the commotion and near pandemonium on the other. The bleating of the nervous sheep was incessant. After spending a whole summer free-range grazing in the broad valleys and verdant hills they were now suddenly confined in an unusual and uncomfortable space. Soon they would be divided and rounded up by their respective owners and transported by truck to be shorn, bred, or sent to market.

Once the unwilling sheep are herded into the common corral, separating them is a true family affair. Hundreds of sheep owned by about 10 different farms have to be individually caught and sorted according to their tags. Parents and rose-cheeked children of any age wade through the flock, grabbing any sheep that bears an appropriate tag or colour and steering them by the horns into their separate corral. Once all have been gathered they are coaxed up a ramp and onto a waiting truck ready to bring them home. At this point the sheep sense something too strange and firmly resist the ramp, hysterically milling about needing some hard shoving before one of them complies to make the first move. Finally, a single sheep breaks rank and quickly tramples up the ramp. Now all hell breaks loose and with a sudden collective change of heart a hundred agitated sheep follow, stampeding up the ramp, crowding and squeezing onto the truck, all in a panic now, afraid to be left behind.

I took the liberty of considering these two sheep as mother and daughter simply because they always moved in unison and had, what I thought at the time, a feminine look. Must have been the facial pink and matching ear tags.

In the fall the annual roundup of sheep is an exciting event producing a continuous racket by man and beast. There is yelling and bleating from dawn till dusk. The abrupt change from freely grazing all summer in the open fields and on green mountainsides to suddenly being tightly squeezed into an unfamiliar confined space with a much taller species has every sheep alarmed. Some are visibly more nervous and agitated, desperately seeking a familiar face while others, like these two black sheep, glare at me with resentful eyes. My concern here was not so much about my camera settings but to make sure that if I lost my balance I was to lose it to the more benevolent side.

After much jostling, bumping and milling about in a tight enclosure, these cozy sheep face in one direction not unlike pennies in a shaken jar or people in a packed elevator.

With a last stare out of the delivery truck, the bleating diminishes and remarkably a quiet resignation sets in.

The wide variety of coloured coats milling about in a tight chaotic formation is as entertaining to watch as a flickering bonfire. Just a few nudges send wavelike motions throughout the crowd like ripples in a pond. It is a continuous domino effect. Some sheep are only tagged while others are both tagged and painted for easier distant identification. Studying these sheep it doesn't take long to discern individual personalities and mannerisms.

Repetition can dull the mind. Go somewhere new.

Many new photographers seem to be fearful of the centre of an image and hesitate to put anything in it. They avoid the centre to the extent that their personal creativity is paralyzed and they feel they are breaking some sort of artistic law. The thinking is that the rule of thirds must apply or else the image has no compositional merit. Adhering to this unfounded principle and being guided by it becomes like painting by numbers, uninvolved, robotic, and unfeeling. Photography is an art and therefore, must totally be subjective reflecting your feelings and emotional connection to the subject and not be dictated by some outward force. Enjoy and do as you please. The only rule in art is that it is the only place in the world where there are no rules.

ICELAND

Meltwater from a hidden glacier.

Thingvellir National Park is one of the most iconic and visited places in Iceland and it is a rare day that one is here alone.

This image was taken at Thingvellir National Park where Iceland's first parliament, the Althing, took place in 930 AD. It is also here that the mid Atlantic ridge is tearing apart and separating the continents of America and Europe at a rate of about 2.5 centimetres a year. This is a walkway that runs inside the fault. To the right is the American tectonic plate and to the left the Eurasian tectonic plate. It is a rare visible part of the mid Atlantic ridge that runs mostly underwater from Greenland to the tip of South America.

After 874 AD, Iceland was becoming settled by so many different families arriving from the Nordic countries that the smaller ones had to rally together to prevent the stronger families from completely dominating this newly settled land. This amphitheatre at Thingvellir was the perfect place for the Icelandic residents to gather. It projected the speakers' voices well and was close to the greatest concentration of families. It is recorded that this was so important that the more remote families would travel 17 days to hear and be heard. This democratic system worked so well that it served as the place of parliament till 1798. Iceland claims that this first coming together was the beginning of their nation.

Standing on the unfolding Eurasian side of the tectonic fault
one looks out towards the east at a wide expanse that is now
a UNESCO World Heritage Site, the Thingvellir National Park.

When I see a vertical wall like this, I am reminded of how tenacious life is. Nature makes a determined attempt to pour life into every crack and cling onto every foothold. Every shell you find on a beach or acorn you gather in the forest seems to have already been touched or chewed. In spite of us, life is pervasive and penetrating. Looking at this picture you are at Thingvellir facing the vertical and extreme edge of the North American tectonic plate. The continental wall that was attached to it is now 40 to 50 feet away, moving behind me in the opposite direction at the rate of a growing fingernail.

After a heavy rain the colours are saturated, accentuating rocks and plants alike.

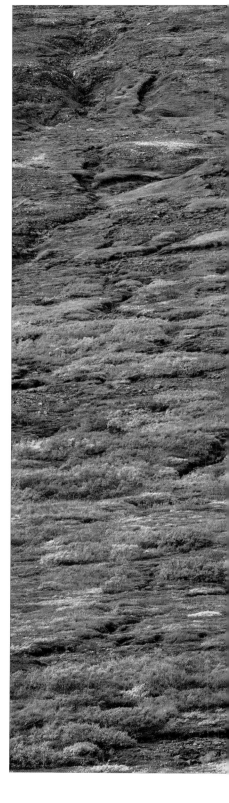

One hundred and fifty centimetres of yearly precipitation erodes a valley and engraves a sloping hillside.

Highland hills of the interior

Volcanic obsidian has a beautiful smooth bluish black sheen that is very different from the usual porous lava rock. Its glassy look is the result of quick cooling preventing it from forming crystals. Even though it is abundant it has an inherent quality attractive enough to make it suitable for ornaments and jewelry.

I normally do not like to shoot on sunny days but I think this time it worked well. Bright highlights and deep shadows on the land and in the snow intricately combine to form an engaging configuration of shapes.

Snow patches on mountain scree

Some days in Iceland the weather is well-balanced and the temperature is quite predictable and calm. Your concerns are not about a drenching rain or a day of blazing sunshine and it makes hiking away from the refuge of your car that much easier. The sky is varied, with clouds coming and going, sometimes building up to a darker grey and then dissolving again into nothing and a deep blue sky reappears. Times like these are welcoming, especially after days of inclement weather.

This image was taken on one of these welcoming days when just a little hope and patience pays off. I purposefully waited for the varying sky to open somewhat to add interest and also to frame the dominant rock. The light was now strong enough to brighten up the black ash and the shadow on the rock, keeping the tones well balanced with the darkened horizon and illuminated landscape.

Washboard roads like these look like an easy drive but after many miles of testing which speed reduces the bone-jarring experience you eventually give up and just accept it as inevitable.

Wind-blasting sand and freezing water has, over the centuries, carved and split this lava mass into the rugged shape it is today.

Hard but brittle, these rocky figures are easily damaged as are the surrounding rocks.

The oxidation of the iron content in this pyroclastic lava gives it a reddish colour.

Iceland is truly a remarkable land of contradictions. One moment you are driving on a smoothly paved road with pastureland on both sides and quite suddenly the luscious greens turn into a strange and unworldly landscape filled with malformed rugged sculptures of lava rock. They look so out of place rising from the boulder-strewn lava field that they can look purposefully made by an alien artist. Experiencing these formations at night when the clouds move under a sliver of moonlight making light and shadows eerily dance about you quickly begin to understand why Icelanders are convinced they could be the malicious works of Loki. Loki is a Norse god that behaves in threatening manners taking on sometimes strange and various shapes. One night here was enough.

Coming down a hillside on this very bright and clear morning it took me a few seconds to make sense of what I was seeing. My eyes wandered over the brown and barren landscape searching for something of interest that would break the uninspiring panorama. As I searched the horizon a bright light, reflected from the snow-covered mountains, burned through the clouds and I realized that what I first took for a clouded horizon was really a stable fog bank trapped over a rough terrain.

I usually do not have much of an empty blue sky in my photographs but this time I thought it was appropriate. The image could have been cropped removing about half of the sky but that would pull the eye down and lead it to consider the foreground which was not my intention. This unconventional composition draws the viewer upward and into the vastness of a clean and boundless landscape. This a good example of how one should be playing to an emotional response and not any guiding rules.

I find this image to be peaceful and very easy to look at. It is a simple image without any jarring elements to disturb the eye. It approximates minimalism, allowing the eye to freely wander. A few billowing clouds hanging over a smooth and undulating terrain work in unison as a clear and uncomplicated landscape.

Minutes before, the entire mountain had been covered in a dense fog with only suggestions of dark shapes and deep shadows as I set up the camera to record the gloomy scene. However, whilst I was preoccupied with changing the batteries the enclosing fog lifted and the melancholy atmosphere was quickly transformed into a more appealing mood with a pleasing mist of green.

All under a wet and cloudy sky Iceland displays an extravagant landscape of glacier-filled mountains, deep valleys of green and skipping waterfalls. Entering a valley such as this an observant photographer can spend days discovering the vast and the intimate.

After an unusually hard rain the landscape took on a very different look. The foreground was saturated and the colours were intense while in the distance the mountains were still dry, retaining their faded monochromatic look. A shaft of sunlight focuses on snow-covered hills.

ICELAND

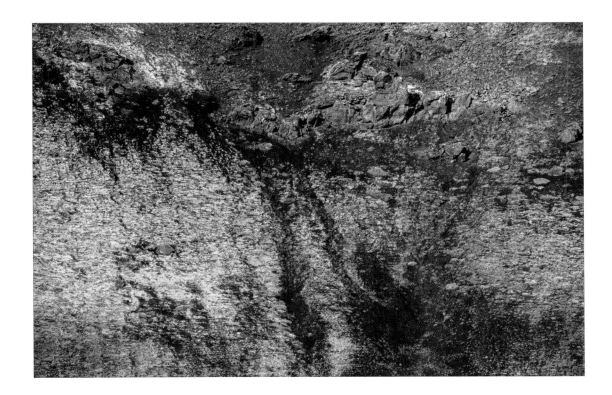

Some landscape photographs can reveal themselves as abstractions. This image is not what might be considered intimate, but is of a distant hillside covered with volcanic ash and yellow moss. Most abstract pictures appear flat and two-dimensional lacking the three-dimensional effect of foreground, middle ground and background.

This image is taken from inside the crater of a volcanic vent that spewed large quantities of purplish cinders forming a small caldera. It is this constant accumulation of ash that gives cone volcanoes their classic inverted V shape. Here this yellow-green moss thrives on a rich supply of minerals and a good supply of water from above and below.

Remnants of last winter linger in deeper valleys and on shaded mountainsides.

The strong contrast between the black ash and white snow set against the distant green moss is a landscape very typical of Iceland.

Composition, light and subject are three of the major factors that affect the success of an image. Even possessing all these prerequisites, some images still might seem like they have failed. A possible reason may be that the viewer, not the photographer, was at fault and did not meet the image halfway. Such doubtful images might require more time and not just a cursory glance. Smaller and more subtle attributes of colour, form, shape and texture must all be considered. Only after being given this fair assessment should a verdict of success or failure be made. It is good to be reminded that the artist must have experienced something that enticed him or her to make the image. Searching and finding these possibly missed qualities can be entertaining and somewhat challenging but if successful can bring an unexpected joy

Overlooking the lava fields at Landmannalaugar where an active volcanic vent spews out hot nauseating gases.

This is a good example of light accentuating the landscape and drawing you in.

This beautiful and nearly vertical wall of ochre-coloured ash is being slowly eroded and washed to the bottom of a ravine. In the spring this loose gravel is carried further downstream by swift rushing meltwater. If you remain quiet and listen carefully you can hear the constant dribbling of individual pieces of ash skipping down this steep incline.

In the days of transparencies it was always a challenge for photographers to expose film properly so that there was detail still left in the whites, such as snow, and not have them blown out without any texture. Depending on the brightness of the day I would take a meter reading off the snow and open the exposure by two or two and a half stops. This made up for the camera's metering system's tendency to try and reduce everything to a neutral grey. With today's digital histogram you can adjust the exposure and visibly see from its information when you are losing detail in the whites. You know immediately if you are correct even before you take the picture and you don't not have to wait for weeks to find out if you were successful.

Sometimes in a photograph volume and shape easily come together to form a unified whole. Unlike other images, where more study is required to compose and understand the randomly scattered objects, this composition is straight forward. A shallow stream ripples through a gravel field and slides between a precipitous slope of hardened rock and an isolated boulder. Immediately you are confronted by a steep and darkly tinted hillside compelling your eye to turn past a patch of snow and deeper into a mysterious valley. The softly coloured hilltops add to the allure and fuel the imagination as to what may lay beyond.

This image of an extinguished vent reminds me of the sense of unease I felt a few years ago when I visited the area around the Reykjanes power installation. I was unexpectedly exposed to the most unnerving sound I have ever heard. This statement cannot be emphasized enough. With the intensity of a nearby jet an extremely loud and deep howling bellowed out of the ground. It sounded like a severely suffering person. This lasted for about five seconds and then, with no change in intensity, turned into a deeper scream of an immense and angry animal. It had no predictable rhythm, pausing a couple of seconds as if to catch its breath, then roaring again in agony. It sounded as if it had an organic source and it did not take much to imagine I was listening to screams emanating from the depths of hell. The continuous blast physically shook me. It was so disquieting that I had to leave. This unnerving event lingered for a long time and gave me a good insight into the immense powers hidden beneath the earth.

Close-up view of a shining stream surrounded by iron-oxide deposits and turquoise-blue rhyolite.

Reminiscent of a primordial place and time.

In the far distance under its usual canopy of clouds, Mount Hekla dominates the landscape with its impressive volume and height, rising 1,500 meters and covering a lava area of 18.5 square kilometres. In the foreground scattered amid the volcanic ash countless lava bombs are strewn about having been ejected for miles demonstrating Hekla's immense power, intensity and capabilities of destruction. It's hard to imagine the energy released from such a gigantic explosion. About 3,000 years ago, Hekla covered the whole of Iceland with ash, an area over 40,000 square kilometres. It seems that such a massive and violent volcano would strike fear in anyone. However, when I spoke with a sheep farmer who had lived all his life under the volcano he just smiled and said that he does not fear it but just lives with it.

II am drawn to this mountain because of its troubling history, its size, and the real threat that it poses today more than ever. Volcanologists are constantly monitoring its activity with great concern. It had erupted with great intensity in 1947 and again with less vigour in 2000. Scientists who study this volcano know that these smaller eruptions and rumblings are just a sign of increased activity, raising the greater potential of a major eruption.

Writers, poets and historians have been drawn to Hekla's reputation as the gateway to hell, where one can hear the wailings and howls of the damned reverberate against the scorching walls of its burning depths. For them it has become the epitome of terror. However dreaded this reputation might be, the locals operating in today's reality just

tap into Iceland's underground hellish activity as their source of renewable and sustainable heat and energy.

One is allowed to climb Hekla on a four kilometre path to the summit. The hike can easily be done but huge warning signs at its base remind hikers of the dangers of the weather quickly turning or of losing one's way through the snowfields. Loud horns situated around the mountain report any unusual volcanic activity and the need for an immediate retreat.

Hekla means cloaked or shrouded. It is a rare day when its snow-and-ash covered crest is visible.

Evening light, Landmannalaugar highlands

Rarely can a photographer say that nature fully cooperated and gifted the perfect light to enhance a landscape that was already captivating and compelling. I had climbed this mountain for a few hours and was excited to be rewarded with such varied and colourful scenery. Everywhere I turned was a display of the unusual. Colours, shapes, patterns, and textures I had never witnessed before filled my viewfinder and I was riveted at every turn. Then the unusual happened. A strong burst of wind blew across where I stood and I saw the distant lower clouds quickly sweep downward and draw across the hills toward, me spreading a fine mist. The light grew dim and the air became so wet I had to shield my camera with a shower cap when unexpectedly a part of the sky opened to brightly illuminate the ground below. The horizon lightened, the moss shone bright green, the hills revealed their colours and the river reflected all of the light. It was a moment I was not prepared for. Instinctively I ripped the plastic from my camera, composed the scene, took a reading of the reflected light, wiped the lens and snapped the shutter.

This simple image demonstrates not only an uncomplicated landscape with an apparent geometric tendency but also highlights the varied reflective colours in the tinted waters of a natural reservoir.

The depth of the washed-out gully in the foreground pays small tribute to the depth of ash that spewed out of Hekla's vents when one becomes aware of the mountain of ash rising hundreds of feet up on the right. Again the mountain is covered in clouds but with much less snow cover compared to the year before. It is these changes that bring me back many times

and with every visit I add to my memories of the landscape. In this panorama the light is quite even and flat, but it is under these conditions that the vivid green moss juxtaposed against the black ash reflects the light best, not having to compete with the strong highlights of a sunny day. The eye is always led to the brightest part of the picture.

The blue hour of this day suddenly turned bright and colourful, transforming the hills of tephra and ash into a brilliant and engaging image. This is what photographers mean when they say they are waiting for the right light. Now warm and cold colours play against each other, drawing you deeper, from a warm foreground up into a bleak and icy horizon.

I am mesmerized by a Martian landscape as an unearthly atmosphere surrounds me. I wandered cautiously among the venting fumaroles and boiling mud pots. Unexpected gurgling sounds rushed up from the fiery world below, caustic odours burned my nose and fumes stung my eyes. Where do I begin?

With no dominant feature this image makes it easy for the eye to slowly wander, discovering subtle colours and harsher textures.

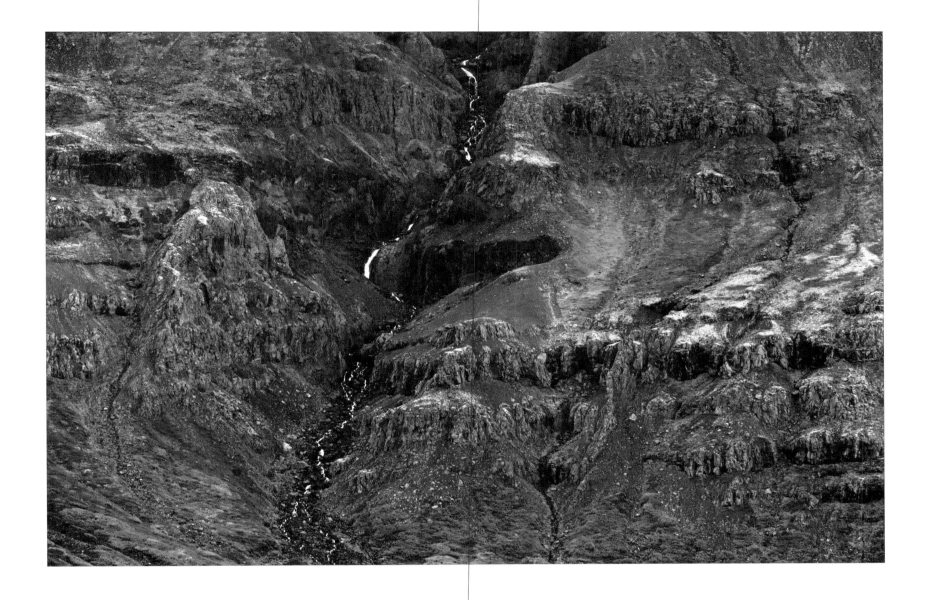

The water from a melting glacier tumbles and spills over numerous rocks and ledges becoming aerated as it filters through the ash below. In Iceland, drinking from the tap is the same as drinking bottled water.

When a low fog sweeps over this rugged scene and washes the lava rock it darkens to a bluish black and turns the moss a brighter green.

What was a few moments ago a flat and nearly monochromatic landscape has, with a wide brush of penetrating light, exposed these hills in their true textures and colours.

Corrosive volcanic fumes coat the rugged mounds in a profusion of distinctive colours: green, cyan, yellow, red and brown.

This phenomenon began with a major volcanic eruption that took place in late 1783 and early 1784. Commonly know as Laki, a 40-kilometre volcanic fissure opened up to expel the largest volume of effluents since the last ice age. Spewing out an unimaginable twelve cubic kilometres of lava covering an area of 565 square kilometres, it also belched out 120 million tons of sulphur dioxide. The gas-choked atmosphere, called the Lakihaze, reflected light and heat back to the sun and the northern hemisphere went cold. Iceland went into a freeze. More than half of Iceland's livestock died of starvation and those that had food died later by ingesting the fodder that was covered with 8 million tons of poisonous hydrogen-fluoride gas. When the acid rain settled it destroyed most of what was growing and famine followed. Ten thousand residents, or 20% of the human population, perished. Much of the countryside was an uninhabitable black desert until this assertive moss took hold and began covering the lava. Volcanic ash is beneficial to the growth of pastureland. Solidified lava 12 metres thick is not.

On the way to the Krafla volcano I stopped by this visually engaging scene of the Krafla Power Plant. It was heartening to see such a clean operation with only white steam as a byproduct. While there I was surprised by the sudden loud explosion of vents releasing pressure from deep underground. The whole volcanic valley filled with a tremendous reverberation that, at first, was concerning but seeing no one running I settled down to make this image.

Iron deposits paint this landscape in a wide swath of ochre, and fumaroles exhale their burning vapours. Underfoot the heat rises and the air is filled with noxious fumes. The stinging gas irritates your eyes and lungs, forcing your breathing to be shallow and measured.

Concentric rings surround the boiling bubbles at Hverir's mud pots, a geothermal area in the northern part of Iceland.

For a photographer it is always a challenge to keep the colours true to the scene. With such a variety of vivid colours around a fumarole one often doubts the outcome of an edited image and is tempted to reduce the saturation so as not to lose an audience's belief in the image. However, I feel it is just as important to convey the true hues emitted by the corrosive mixture of volcanic gases.

Confusion in a space always draws the eye to the simple form that is better understood. In this case it may be the swirl of yellow orange on top, the dark stripe boldly cutting across the image or the brighter reddish patch below.

140

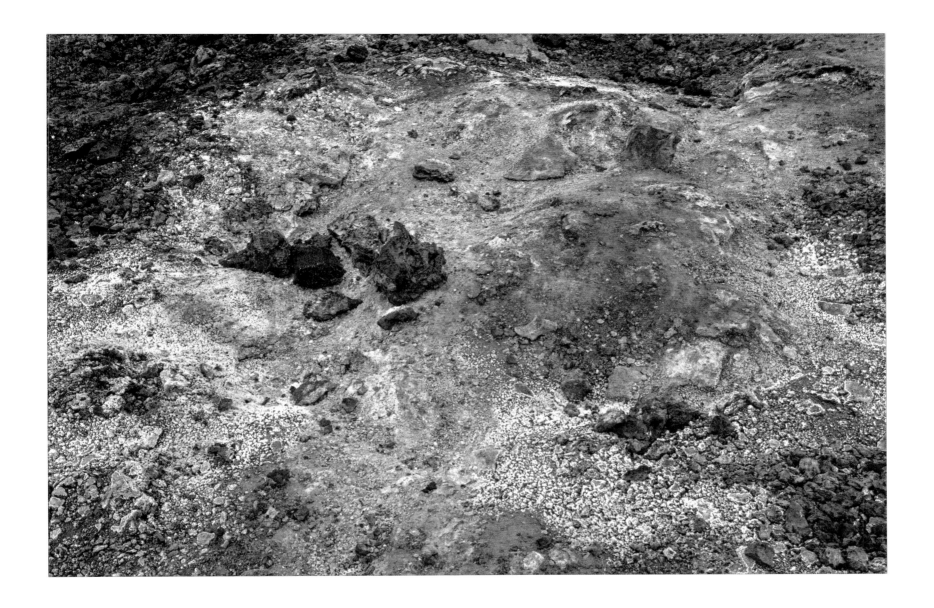

A well-known photographer once said, semi jokingly, that to photograph well one must know where to stand. Another said that all one needs to know is where to point the camera. Yet another said that one only has to know where to put the four corners in a photograph. So, to make sure I succeeded, I heeded the advice of all three. I walked till I figured this was the best place to stand and since the subject was below me that's where I pointed the camera and I leaned in back and forth till all the corners were just right.

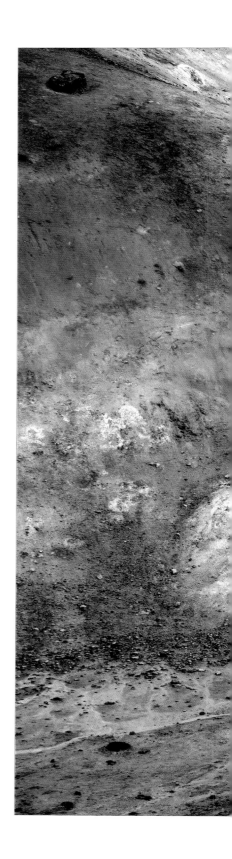

As a photographer I am intrigued by colour, texture and form, so when I happened on this scene, I could hardly contain my excitement. Deciding how to compose this compelling photograph became the burning issue.

ICELAND

TThe approach to photography and to painting is somewhat different. A painter begins with a blank canvas and methodically builds up each section bit by bit adding to the composition. The landscape photographer, on the other hand, begins with a finished image. He must visualize what part of the landscape is significant to his vision and then go about eliminating the various elements that detract and keep those that do not. Leaving something in or out can make or break the aesthetics of the picture. The photographer is as responsible for the whole image surface as the painter is for his whole canvas. Both have an artistic vision and intent. In photography images that do not recognize this intent become snapshots.

The main subject, sitting boldly on the horizon against a neutral sky, is a dark cinder cone, while in the foreground carefully positioned orange bushes add balance and depth. An even greater feeling of depth is realized when one notices the distant hills on the left seemingly sinking below the horizon.

In some places in Iceland, far from anything remotely familiar, it's easy to imagine yourself a visiting astronaut landed on a primordial planet on the verge of just cooling down enough to allow primitive life to establish itself. All is moist, dark and gloomy. The light is strange, and the atmosphere has a stinging array of unfamiliar odours. Amongst the irritating reek, the only odour recognizable would be the sharp one of burning sulphur. All around you the steaming mist rises and its humidity warms your face. Bending to touch the rock you find its conductive heat surprising. It feels like touching the back of a big animal. You slowly realize that you are now standing on a crust of cooling lava just as the whole earth was billions of years ago. Here in Iceland you can step back in time.

From this primordial blend of microbes, algae, heat and water, life pushed forward to what we are today.

A well-used trail runs along this steep hillside of volcanic ash and across last year's snowfield. That morning I had crossed this melting and decaying snow bridge but only now, after seeing it from another hill, did I fully realize what a dangerous and weakened crossing it was. An undermining stream from its melting snow runs below it, forming an ever-weakening snow bridge. It may be fortunate that I did not take the darker well-used trail but stayed higher up and scrambled across a thicker and stronger section of the bridge. Crossing it has become an unknowing game of chance where a total collapse is inevitable.

Still steaming with heat coming from its fissures, this active volcano is constantly being monitored for any signs of rumbling and increased underground activity. The dangers these Icelandic volcanoes pose are extensive not only for the people of Iceland but also for the very vulnerable countries of Europe. Britain especially is in a critical position being close and directly in the path of the prevailing winds that would carry the razor-edged particles of ash and other toxic pollutants into its atmosphere. Spewed thousands of feet into the airspace of planes flying at blistering speeds these minute pulverized fragments of ash can abrade fuselage and windshields and then melt in the engines causing total engine failure. The recent eruption of the Eyjafjallajokull volcano in 2010 was a tangible warning of what Western Europe must plan and be prepared for.

Tricky to walk over, this lava field can easily cause one to stumble. If it is not green it is rock, and no matter how soft and gravelly it looks, it has no give. Hiking boots catch readily with their built-in grip, and when carrying heavy equipment a fall can be damaging to camera and body alike. I had scrapes and bruises to prove it.

An arctic sun paints the Eldhraun moss with a wide brush transforming the dull colours of autumn into a rich and radiant gold. In the shaded areas the moss retains more of its natural colours of yellow, black, grey, and brown.

A fluid curve of dark stones leads the eye into this magnificent scenery of open tundra, rugged mountains and crumbling glacier. Avoiding as much as possible walking on this fragile terrain, I followed this dried rivulet, fascinated by the appeal of the surrounding colours, textures and patterns. Seemingly overlooking a miniature fall forest, I studied the variety and diverse arrangements of the low-lying flora. A sudden blast of cold wind descended from the immense glacial plateau bringing with it a cool fog, blanketing the entire landscape with a nurturing mist.

Although well-watered and well enriched by the crumbling lava, few plants can break through this thick, thriving growth of moss.

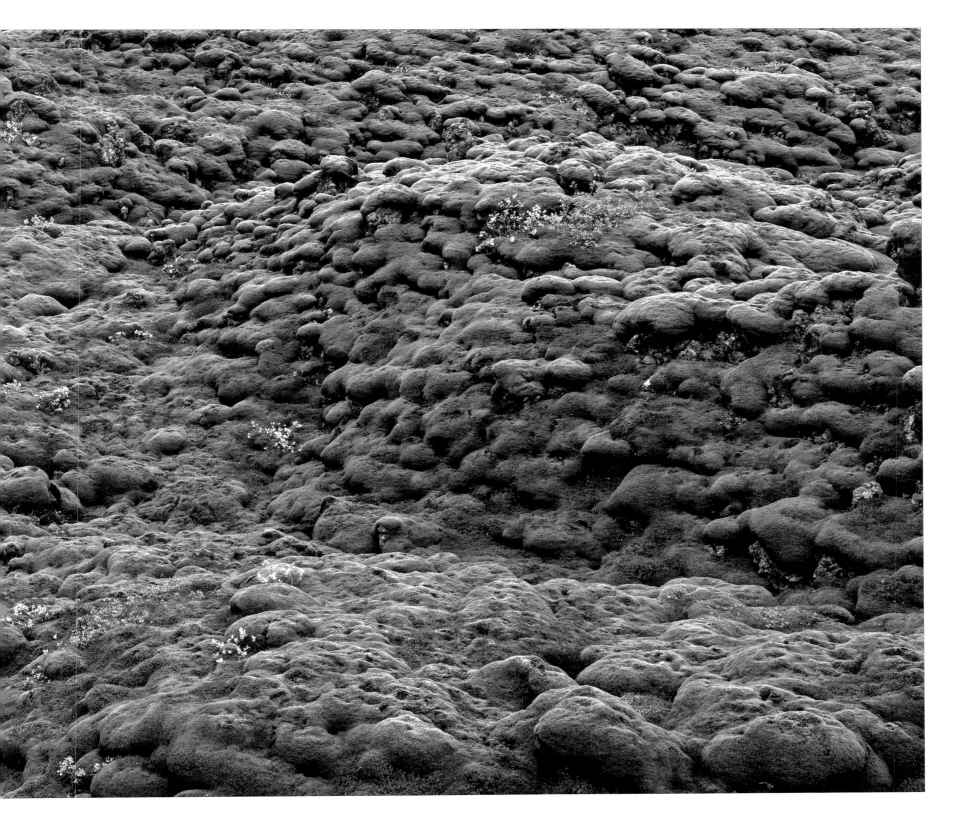

This was not an easy composition to decide on. The scene had many distinctly coloured and textured features spread out at different distances. There was rippling water in the foreground and a cloudy sky in the background with a vibrant and varying terrain in between. I was limited in where I could stand, so the choice of what to include or exclude in the image had to be made here. At first I considered not including the water in the foreground but that would only pull the eye upward to the snow-covered mountain and out of the picture. My other option was to exclude the sky but that would draw the eye downward to the brighter water. Neither of these options would bring the focus of attention to the colourful and highly textured middle ground. I decided to keep both the brighter snow and the reflecting water making the image more balanced, settling the eye on the more important and engaging middle ground. As you study the image more closely you become aware of the two very different hillsides funnelling a more recent lava flow that stops abruptly in front of a small eroding knoll and black sandy beach.

Not only is this image a display of a tortured land with mountains and moss-covered lava in upheaval, but also one of tone and texture. The subtle tones of blue in the distant hills and the delicate shades of yellow and green in the fragile moss raise this picture from what could easily have been a black and white image into a coloured one. Each colour is reserved and of even tone, keeping its visual attention to a minimum and understated. This undisturbed tonality allows the eye to wander and explore the texture and feel of the land.

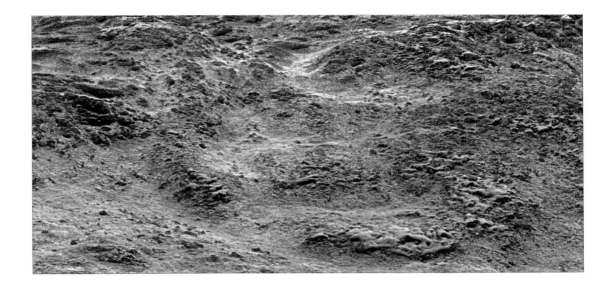

Scenes of broad hillsides covered in green and yellow mosses interspersed with red berry leaves have become for me signature landmarks of Iceland.

Red pyroclastic lava at the opening of a volcanic vent

I had not expected this, but only a few minutes from the international airport at Keflavik you are already in a landscape that is barren and unfamiliar.

It will be many years before the cooling earth gives up its magma and the blistering lava ceases to flow over Iceland.

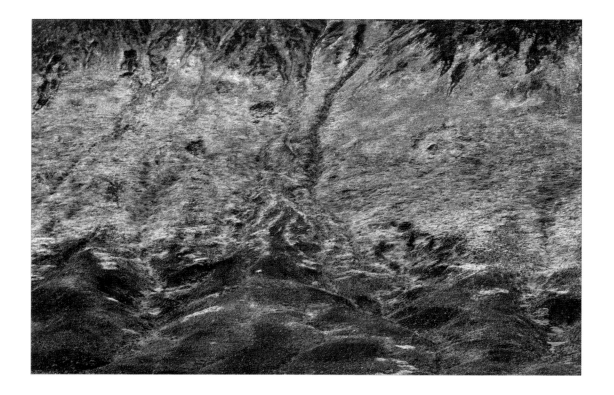

Sandy in appearance, these hillsides of volcanic ash have, over the millennia, coalesced into an enduring rock. It takes many years for rivulets to carve their individual paths.

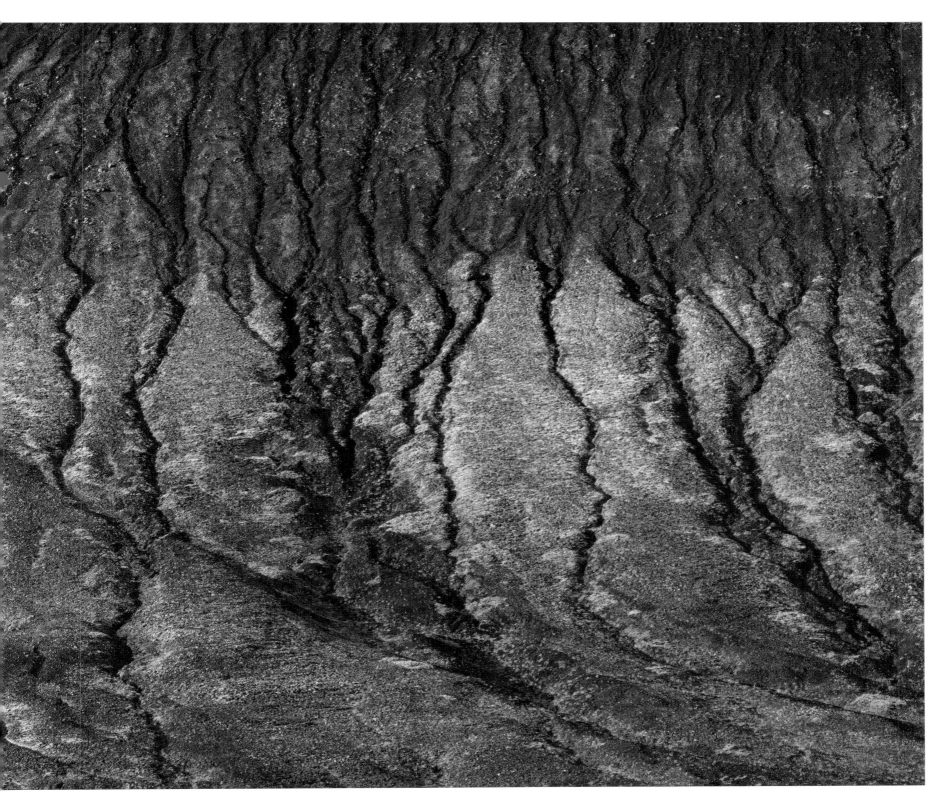

In a minimalist image there are only a few elements that are the focus of attention. In these two there are but three: the rippled sand, the grass and the cloudy sky. They are not complicated pictures and you have no doubt as to what you should be looking at. To make such an image successful it is good practice to examine especially the perimeter of the image for any possible disturbing elements that would distract the eye and take away the attention from the main subject, in this case the rippled sand.

ICELAND

Pebbles on the beach at Vestrahorn

This low-hanging fog over the headland of Stokksnes can leave many one-time visitors frustrated, wishing to see its top in full sunshine. I have spoken with photographers who have waited for days in hope of catching a glimpse. It is one of Iceland's most visited and iconic scenes. Not wishing to see an empty blue sky I was relieved to be without the crowds and happy with the descending fog.

A profusion of vigorous plants have established themselves on a rising mound of fertile ash.

This image was taken from the right side of the road as you descend a steep hill entering the well-known town of Vik. Tourists visit by the thousands and this day was no different. The traffic was at a halt and people milled about their cars waiting for the unseen issue to be resolved. I walked a bit and studied the lush variety of green plants that covered the hillside. Suddenly I realized what an opportunity this was and pulled out the tripod to compose this unplanned and unexpected landscape. Moments like this are rare but they definitely elevate your spirit.

The main roads of Iceland are all well-maintained.

In the distance the white snowy peak stands out distinctly against a saturated blue sky. At these elevations the light can be intense as seen in the blue reflection in the snow patch on the right.

Finally the sky over this landscape was what I had hoped for. This was my fourth time travelling along this well-maintained dirt road and I was fascinated by how it was deeply entrenched into the sweeping plain. I wanted to take a picture of it but every time I passed this way the sky was an empty deep blue or the sun was shining directly into the camera. Having many years experience with a large format 4 x 5- inch camera where there was a cost for every image I took, I quickly learned not to take an image unless it was exactly what I wanted. Even though I now shoot digitally this approach still applies. Hence the long wait to make this picture. Fortunately, on this last passing, the light that penetrated a thickly clouded sky was even and subdued, revealing the many earthy tones of the road, hills and grasses. Enveloped in this muted light the image now has a softer look with an even tonality that allows all the elements to be visible and fill the picture.

ICELAND

Iceland's paved roads meander smoothly over a wide and open landscape. With such a solidified base I do not recall ever dealing with a pothole or a bump.

ICELAND

The most important part of the picture is its centre. Its success all depends on what you put in it. Masses of blue lupins contrast with the patches of yellow providing a welcome visual relief.

A tundra swan glides across this arctic lake. In spring this road is underwater.

Even though it is evening, what photographer would want to leave this place now and try to get back to a hotel? The possibility of what might be missed is just too much. I had no intention of taking this image but on my way back after an hour of wandering under a very cloudy sky the moss-covered hill lit up brightly, and for a few passing minutes, completely changed the feeling of the place. The single beam of light moved slowly towards me, washing over the hill, touching the water. This picture is a good example of how a massive mountain and a small car, objects so different in size, can compete for attention.

A narrow road runs through a small lava field and along a meandering river. In the distance a misty sky covers some of the lakes and mountains that make up Fjallabak Nature Reserve.

ICELAND

Quite unexpectedly I once again had to use my tripod as a defense mechanism. The previous time my tripod came in very handy was in Antarctica when somehow I had annoyed a pair of very aggressive skuas who began dive bombing me persistently, hitting me hard on the head. I could not see them coming because their attacks came directly out of the sun. My solution was to open my tripod and hold it upside down over my head like overgrown antennae and keep moving along at a steady pace. Eventually, out of nest range, I was left alone but a little more wary of whose place this was. This time in Iceland, crossing a field trying to find my way to some basalt columns, I met this threatening sheep with diabolical eyes that would not let me pass. Amused, I took his picture. Not seeing it my way he charged with head down and it was with this first attack that the jousting with horns and tripod began. After four or five attempts at reaching me, he moved on to join the others. Needless to say, the message was received and my return journey took a different route.

Deceptive in appearance these tiny looking waterfalls are approximately ten feet wide.

This is a detailed view of the Jokulsargljufur canyon where all the grey-white water of the great Dettifoss waterfall rushes through. The thick and heavy spray is forced up by the displaced air and is driven against the canyon walls, accumulating in small streams and rivulets flowing down to the maelstrom below. This was late autumn and water flow was minimal. During the spring thaw the canyon is filled from side to side, covering all the rocks below, becoming the biggest waterfall in Iceland.

This image may not be a crowd pleaser but it is a good example of how the Icelandic fog envelopes the sponge-like moss soaking it enough to keep it green and growing. The bloated lumps are in some places over a foot thick, deceptively hiding small rocks and spanning the deeper and larger spaces between them. Hundreds of years in the making but you still get an over-enthusiastic tourist rolling or jumping across this fragile covering, marring the expanse for decades.

In photography looking up is just as important as looking down.

Infused with cyan a glacier tongue spills over a cliff of hardened ash

Melting faster than its push forward this slowly deteriorating tongue of ice is part of Iceland's southernmost glacier. Situated north of the town of Vik, Myrdalsjokull is an icecap 596 square kilometres in area and covers the infamous and worrisome Katla volcano. Long past its expected and somewhat predictable eruption date, it is Iceland's greatest concern. Continuous tremors indicating lava movement and a rising of the rivers of melted ice forewarn of the beginning of a possible major eruption. In 2011 a subglacial eruption melted enough ice to cause a serious flood, washing out a bridge on the Icelandic ring road, preventing access to the rest of the island. Today this route is fully repaired and bridges have been replaced or strengthened. Anticipating another possible eruption, volcanologists continue to closely monitor Katla's restless activity.

At the bottom of this picture black ash is covered by dark green and yellow mosses giving it a sombre look. However, moving up into the image the picture brightens to complete white with no texture or colour. The moisture coming off this massive area of ice becomes covered with a nearly perpetual fog making it one of the wettest locations in Iceland. Mosses love it.

Under an opening sky Baula mountain extends its gentle slopes to a farm below. While I waited for the light to illuminate the scene, I decided to make the image into a panorama, giving it a cinematic effect that I thought more effective than a tighter crop. I did take a closer image but this one conveys more effectively the grandeur of the landscape and surrounding vista.

Sheep graze in a natural pasture of vivid green and bundles of fodder are ready for another season. When I see scenes as these, I come to the conclusion that Iceland and Greenland should switch names.

While exploring and travelling through vast expanses of volcanic ash, mountainous terrain, and lava fields, you can suddenly come upon unexpected tracts of lush green fields nourished by fertile sands and dedicated hard-working farmers. Committed to such a lifestyle, one must fully accept and bear the isolation and loneliness that such conditions can bring.

This iconic sea stack is the strong and obvious focal point in this picture and is so because of its prominence and isolation surrounded by a flat beach and level sea. Fortunately, the sky is heavy with darkened clouds and the blackened mountains on the far horizon are muted and removed, while a hint of an emerging light brightens the waves and the column of rock. Seabirds profit from the safety of the top and in return supply the flourishing plants with an ample supply of much-needed nutrients.

In autumn the southern coast of Iceland bears the brunt of North Atlantic storms arriving unimpeded from as far away as the equator.

The time I most prefer exploring the seaside is on an overcast day when the light is even and the receding tide has left a wet beach with a new jumble of flotsam. As much as a mountain view can be dramatic, it is for the most unchanging except for the weather covering it or over a longer period with the colours of the seasons. The beach, on the other hand, offers tides twice daily, challenging a photographer's vision and creativity to fill a viewfinder with compelling shapes and exciting colours all balanced into an absorbing and intriguing design.

If you are a person who loves to get down on hands and knees to study and explore smaller fauna then Iceland provides an ample variety. With over 5,000 species of trees, shrubs, flowers, mosses and lichens merging in all sorts of combinations of colours, shapes and textures, spots like these are visual treasures. Every square foot is a world unto its own just waiting to be explored. If one paid attention to all the detail it would be a vortex of time before a small area such as this could be covered. At home we can plan and work our artificial gardens into any shape or form as much as we want, but nothing can compare to nature's profusion and aesthetic qualities. In our gardens we are consciously or unconsciously imitating what nature has always done not only first but better.

Situated in the north-eastern part of Iceland, the lowlands around lake Myvatn are home to a great number of bird species that gather here yearly to breed and raise their young. Unfortunately they are also the breeding grounds for midges. On my first visit I did not know this, nor did I expect to be harassed by these small two-winged flies that immediately sense your presence and invade all exposed areas of your body. So quick are they to explore your eyes, ears, nose and mouth that they make photography nearly an impossibility. Fortunately, unlike the mosquito, they do not bite but just irritate and distract, insisting on and demanding all your attention. I should have known better. *Myvatn* means Midge Lake.

On this day the darkened sky opened up periodically and spotlighted various parts of the scene. I had all the calibrations made to take a picture of a darkened and more sombre landscape when a much brighter light suddenly covered the foreground, changing it dramatically, highlighting the green moss, giving it a more saturated hue. To maintain this now brighter colour and not have it overexposed I recalibrated my readings and shortened my exposure time. By chance, in the distance, the image also captured a mass of bright midges whirling over the lake.

When you come across such a soft carpet of colours, you cannot help but feel a certain degree of guilt as you gingerly try and step through it, knowing full well that no matter how careful you try to be you are going to damage something that took hundreds of years to become established. I circumnavigated many of these fragile barriers, stopping often to study what I came to photograph. On rainy days when overcast skies and shadows have softened, each leaf and twig takes on a deeper hue. It is in moments such as these, when you clearly see the beauty of all the tints and shades of the colour spectrum, that you begin to fully appreciate and realize what a wonderful gift colour vision is.

This very seductive road draws you through fertile fields of lupins into a volcanic countryside.

Photography is a very personal art form that allows you to create an image of something that has touched you. There is something special and distinctive about the moment you press the shutter. This becomes the point at which you take the image to heart and make it yours. It has a very fulfilling and satisfying feeling. Even though iconic places or attractions are worth seeing and experiencing firsthand I rarely photograph them. They are like fast food in the photography world, readily available and prepackaged. However, having said all that, I am sometimes guilty and go against what I feel and succumb to the strong attraction of the popular and iconic destinations such as this church at Vik on the southern coast of Iceland. Viewing it from a distance I was drawn not so much to the red and white but more to the surroundings of bright pervasive greens, hills of mottled brown and distinct patches of blue. Photographs reflect how you felt at the moment.

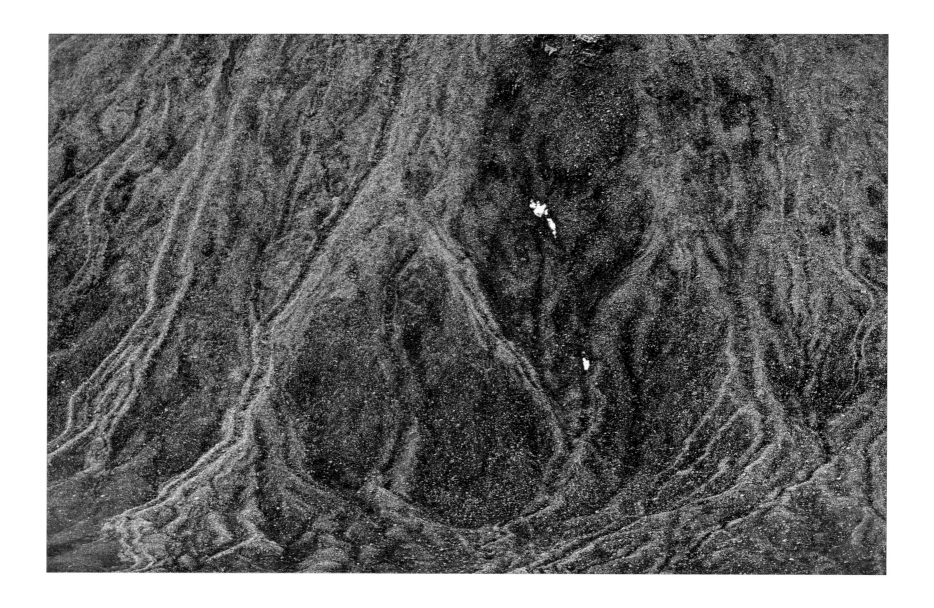

Traces of heavy rains leave meandering patterns flowing down mountains of volcanic ash. Seasonal weathering can remove the different layers of multicoloured ash adding to and changing our impressions of the landscape.

Appreciated by thousands of hikers from around the world, the Landmannalaugar region of Iceland has much to offer in trails, cabins, and colourful scenery. Here two trekkers pause to rest, admire the view, and, I have no doubt, are grateful to witness such a compelling and colourful landscape.

In a five minute drive the landscape can change dramatically. Add to that a sudden change in weather and the scene you thought so banal and colourless has become exciting and vibrant. So driving in huge circles on different days may not be as pointless as it first seems. The land at no time seems to repeat itself. It is like stepping into a flowing river, never stepping into the same water twice.

210

I like working alone. It allows me to slow down, appreciate what I am seeing, and not feel any pressure to say something or move on. I can stand before a scene for as long as I need without distractions. Only then do I feel I can concentrate on what I am seeing and try to meet it halfway.

An early spring drizzle saturates and darkens the colours of an exposed hillside. How else besides a picture can one truly describe the variety and complexities of the intense shades, tints and colours that this painterly landscape exhibits?

It is remarkable how the type of cloud can affect the quality of light that covers the landscape.

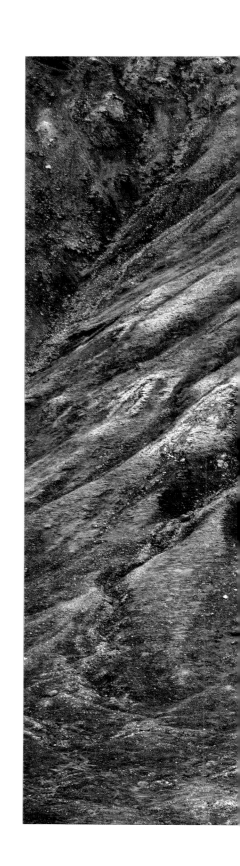

Some of Iceland's most compelling hills display an artist's palette with a ready-painted abstraction.

ICELAND

Finally, sunrise, and there is enough light to bring out the colours of the landscape. When I travel repeatedly to the same country or location I like to stagger the time of year to discover the different moods and qualities that each season brings. Experiencing Iceland in the spring can be more productive because the days are so much longer. In the late fall when you sleep in the car or tent you are very limited with what you can do because the sun goes down very early, around 7:00 p.m., and rises around 7:30 a.m. There is a lot of reading and reflection that can be done but it also becomes a struggle to try and stay awake. Doze off early and you are guaranteed to be all slept out at four or five in the morning with another two or three hours to wait for the sun to appear. If it happens to be an overcast sky or if it is raining then the wait is longer still.

217
ICELAND

ICELAND

As a photographer I do not hesitate to return to the same places. Before I took this picture I had travelled this road a few times, parked the car, and walked over the lava field trying to find a satisfying image of this ski hill. There was something compelling about it but somehow things did not come together either in composition or in light so I did what I learned to do and that was to just walk away. This time the low misty clouds gave off a soft and diffuse light adding texture to the dust-covered snow, which contrasted sharply with the blacks that covered the surrounding hillside with a strong mottled design. Stepping out of the car I did not have to go far to set up my tripod. Instead of using a few moss-covered lava rocks as foreground I decided to use the glistening road as a leading line. This was made all the more effective by the bright and deeply saturated guideposts.

One of Iceland's most iconic landmarks, the snowfield on Snaefells shines with a blazing light. It was popularized by Jules Verne in his science fantasy book, "*Journey to the Center of the Earth*". There are now snowmobile tours to its summit re-enacting in part the novel's characters' first steps into the volcano and onto the path that would lead them into the depths of the earth.

I was driving on the Snaefellsnes (Snow Mountain Peninsula) to see the Snaefellsjokull (Snow Mountain Glacier) on Snaefell (Snow Mountain).

Evenly scattered lava bombs on a plain of volcanic ash and dust.

Photography is about what you see and not what the camera sees. I see a line of grey boulders weaving across a grey lifeless slope distinctly separated from a wet and verdant cliff. It is a fine example of how tenuous life can be.

Looking like crackled glass, this rock face becomes dry twice a day. Now at low tide, the polished surface reflects the colours of the water and the sky.

Tiny streams of water pour down these pigmented basalt steps that resemble stones of an ancient ruin.

This is a complex picture that needs to be lived with and studied for a while in order to become more familiar with all its components. The illumination that highlights the tumbling water is especially intriguing in the way it glances off the edges of this sharply angled stone.

The lower half of this image would normally be underwater but it was late in the fall and the river level had fallen significantly. I was fortunate to be able to photograph the texture of the highly water-polished basalt on the lower levels and compare it to the more angular basalt higher up.

ICELAND

230

Mostly hexagonal in structure, these fitted columns reflect this rock's most basic molecular structure.

232

This image is all about form, light, texture, colour and movement. The elegant sway of the unusual bent columns of basalt rock leaning heavily against the upright pillars adds rhythm, tension, and life to the image. In the early spring the lower section of this wall is inundated with a strong torrent of meltwater that scours the rock clean of plants and pigments. The base of the smoother well-washed surfaces now reflect a softer blue from a cloudless summer sky. And above, rocky pigments, bright fungus, and white guano cling to one of nature's most compelling and captivating designs. With a little imagination one could call this an action shot, albeit a very slow one.

One of the advantages of taking pictures of rivers and streams in the Arctic is that composition is not compromised by windfall and awkwardly lying logs that would be too conspicuous and draw away the attention that should be directed to the greater landscape. The beauty in this simple scene is in the combination of the countless textures in the rock, the varied colours of green, the patterns in the water surface and a cloud-filled sky.

This moss along this riverbank has a very short growing season, especially when one considers that in the spring it is mostly under water.

I am standing on a moss-covered hillside looking over a dappled landscape. In the far distance and much higher in altitude, the hills are still covered in ice and snow. Climbing these hills is always a visual discovery.

On a very steep collapsing cliff, round volcanic rocks find the base and the finer dust and powders cling to form an abstract hanging curtain. Above this a textured wall of coloured shapes is freshly exposed, in stark contrast with the smooth and blended form below.

Carving through steep-walled gullies, streams from the snowy highlands flow into a deeper valley below.

A lava field and braided river in Landmannalaugar

Late summer still has remnants of last winter's snow and volcanic vents puff out their fumes of the netherworld. Volcanic dust and ash spread by mountain winds loosely cover the ice fields, reminiscent of a watercolour painting.

I was having an uncomfortable night filled with intermittent sleep when the alarm went off. It was 5:00 a.m. Tired and sore from yesterday's long hike I now felt reluctant to fulfill my plans for today, but I knew better and began my breakfast ritual of peanut butter on a bagel washed down with some bottled tap water.

It had been a cold night so I was not surprised to see fresh snow covering the higher peaks. The day looked promising with a flat moody light that better suited the dark inky landscape. I did not want a blue sky nor a washed-out grey that a blazing sun can create. My plan today was a moderate climb up Brennisteinsalda, an 835-meter hill of ash and lava. After a slippery two hour scramble over loose volcanic scree and with the darker subdued light still holding I was rewarded with this compelling scene.

In the near middle of this image you can follow the winding trail that leads upward to the blue-black summit of Blahnjukur or Blue Peak. On the horizon are the snow-covered peaks of the Landmannalaugar highlands.

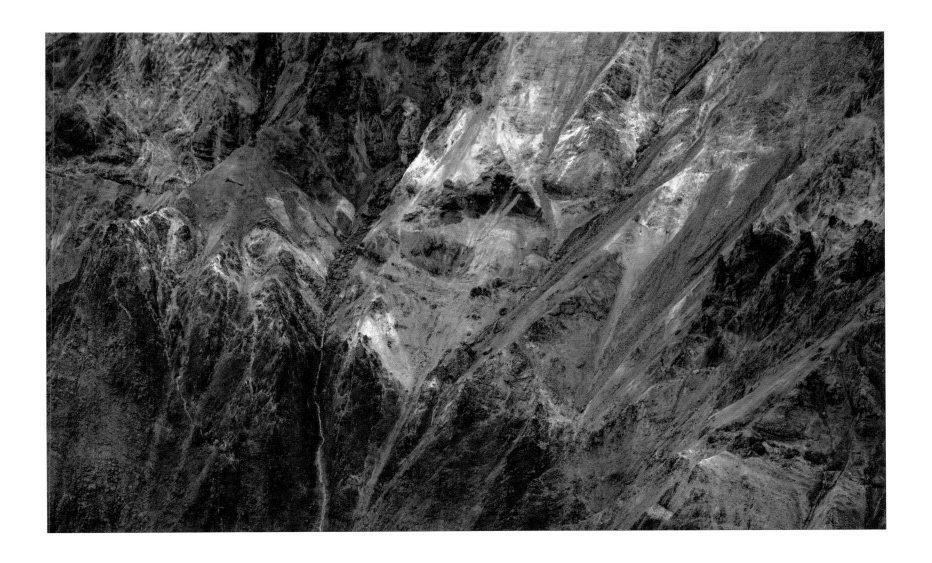

Looking through a camera's viewfinder funnels all your attention, forcing you to search for a composition of colour, line and texture.

Removed of its overburden by gravity and weathering, this crumbling mountain reveals an interior of ochre-coloured ash.

245

These hills were not built by an upheaval of the land but by an accumulation of ash in a titanic explosion that blew billions of tons of rock across a hundred square kilometres.

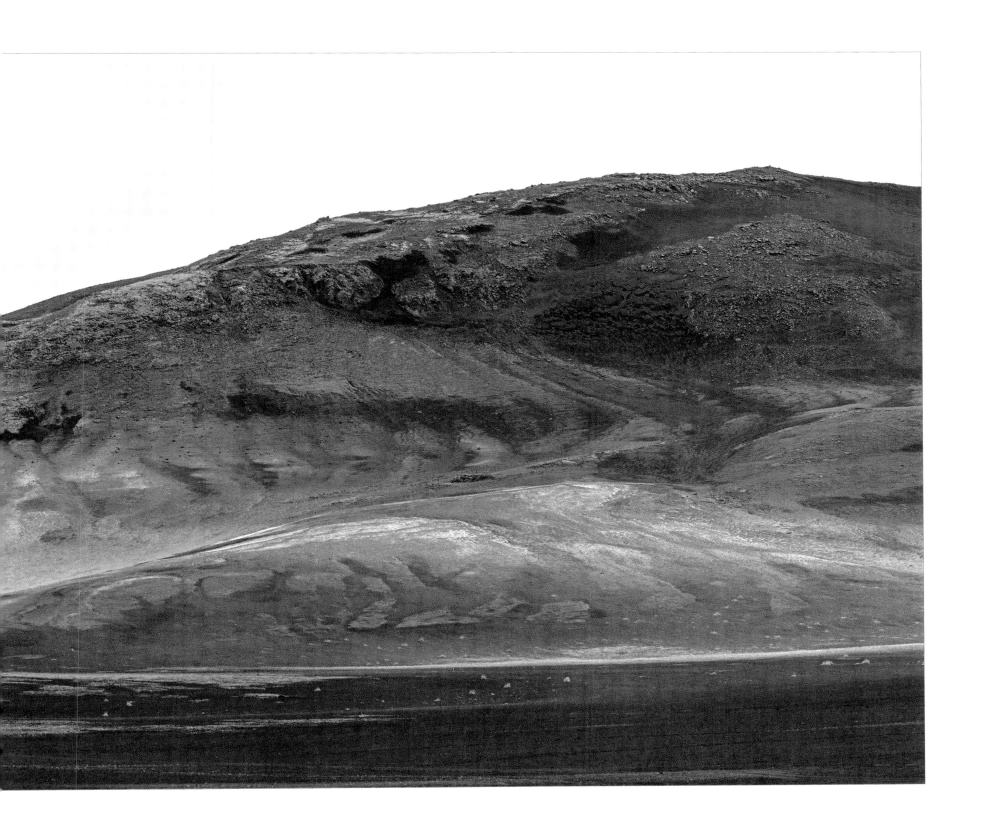

ICELAND

248

Sometimes it is best to keep an image simple and let it tell the story.

This compressed embankment of ash has, over the millennia, resisted the erosion of gravity and water. If Antarctica is known for its whites, Iceland surely must be known for its blacks.

It is no wonder the astronauts Neil Armstrong and Buzz Aldrin spent time here training for their moon landing.

The landscape of Iceland can be austere, severe, and cold. However, in this case the opposite is true. Not only was the temperature of this day agreeable but the steam rising from a volcanic vent and the attractive yellow-green of the moss in the foreground brought forth a feeling of warmth and comfort. In the receding distance a rugged lava field that once was part of nature's most heated spectacles lies softened by the sun, and a blue summer sky fills the horizon.

A leading line, like this moss-covered trough, is an effective way to draw the viewer deeper into the image and on to the highlands beyond.

The sheet of ice covering this 1,500 metre high mountain is Iceland's most southern glacier. It conceals a part of Katla, a massive and active volcano that experts fear is soon to erupt. In 2011 the intense heat from the volcano melted enough ice to discharge enormous volumes of water mixing it with ash to create a slurry that extended the shoreline nearly five kilometres out to sea. Iceland is still increasing in size.

Most people in Iceland live in the capital city of Reykjavik. Others choose to live in the 20 percent of the land that is habitable. Although remotely located and separated by mountains, valleys and fjords they are serviced with well-maintained roads.

Harbour at Grunddarfjodur

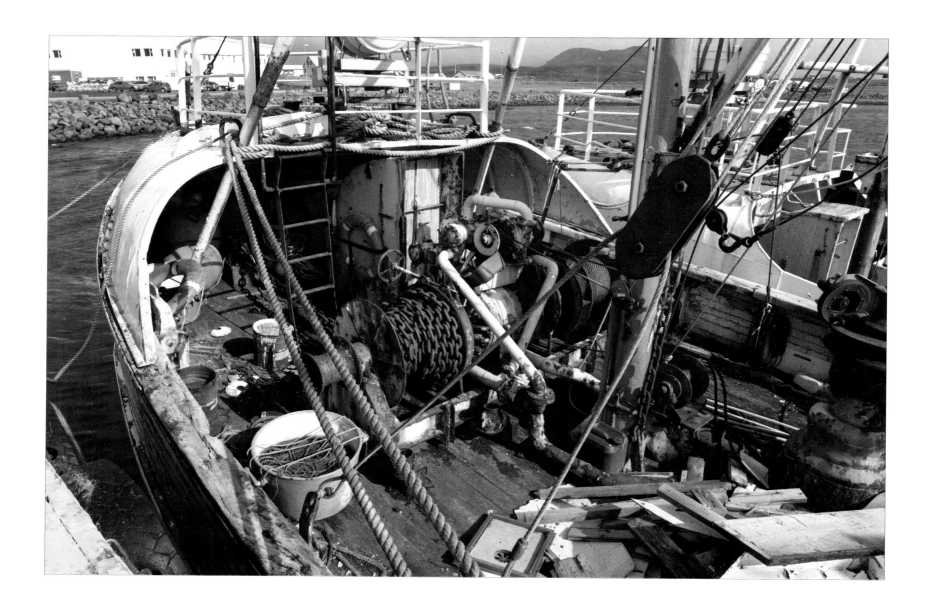

When I look at all the images that I've taken over the years I often wonder how much I would remember without them. It has been proven that when one recalls a place or event it really is just a memory of a memory and not the actual event. Over time, as these recollections are repeated, some suitable imagination enters the picture replacing the inevitable gaps. Eventually it all grows so distorted that it becomes more of a feeling than the real occurrence. Fortunately, images like family photographs preserve the real and help revive these moments. Thanks to photography we can jog our memory as to what our babies looked like. Or are we still fooled and just remembering a picture of our child and not the child itself? Even then we may not be sure which child it is. In the days before photography if your children were not painted or sketched what would you remember of them?

Without any permission to climb aboard, I could not find any meaningful composition from my point of view to express the disastrous state of this dilapidated deck. Even the old rusting hull of the boat looked so alarmingly neglected that I felt it should not even be afloat. Reluctant to give in to my vision of a sunken boat I experimented with a compilation of this derelict by digitally adding water and a picture of fish I had taken before. The image now has the tenuous look of an underwater wreck.

When the Norse arrived in Iceland and entered this bay they saw the land covered in smoke. With no inhabitants and no trees to burn this surely must have been the vapours spewing out of fumaroles. So they called it Reykjavik or Smoky Bay.

I came across these two deteriorating and abandoned boats in Grindavik harbour on the south coast of Iceland. I was immediately taken by their patina and rusting textures as well as by the reflections they made. The possibility of a few more images here seemed promising and I methodically scanned the vessels for real and abstract pictures. The trouble was that everything I wanted to take was inaccessible. I could not walk around the boats nor climb aboard. A little frustrated I made a few more images and paced some more when a voice behind me asked what I was waiting for. I turned to see an older gentleman smiling and inviting me to get on board his boats. He told me he was meaning to restore them and take out tourists for trips around the harbour. He sensed that I seemed to doubt his words so he tried to reassure me by jumping on board and pointing out all the notable features. I returned three years later and the boats were there, surprisingly still afloat.

A fluorescent yellow beam, a rusty orange cleat, a bright cyan hawser and a various-coloured hull all add to the visual confusion at this dockside.

The strength in this picture comes from the impact of bright yellow hovering over a complementary dark blue. Conspicuously dead centre against the darker background it instantly becomest the primary subject. Even though the background is secondary it has a well-balanced colour scheme, tonality and texture. The hints of green, yellow and red are well muted and do not deter from the main subject. The coarse rusty quality of the hull effectively masks both ends of the hawser, leaving the yellow section well pronounced. On the bottom left, a dark iron plate visually anchors the yellow hawser and the welded seams of rusting iron are positioned in a pleasing grid-like distribution. This image is a good example of how much a supportive background determines the success of the main subject.

It took about six hours before I was able to take this picture. I had studied all the interesting portholes of this ship but these were the four that attracted me the most. One was blue, one yellow, one white and the fourth was welded shut. They were then just about knee high above the side of a wharf, but too low for a picture. Their awkward position would not give me an effective composition. It was when I heard a strong grinding of the ship's hull against the wharf and I realized there was some tidal activity. By the look of things it was low tide. I would return for high tide when the portholes would be raised and more visible. Five hours later when I returned the ship had risen a bit too much for a planned wide-angle shot. I now would have to point upwards which would have given the image a disturbing keystone effect throwing all things out of proportion. To solve the problem I stepped further back and used a longer lens to bring it into a truer direct perspective.

An abstract image is not for everyone, but if one lives with it, studies it, and views it long enough, it is quite surprising what it will reveal. All images do not divulge their attributes easily.

Smaller images can sometimes suggest more than a larger one. What is the story behind these hawsers? Where have they been? Who handled them? Where else will they go or is this the end of the line?

Having just arrived in Iceland my first stop was the close harbour town of Grindavik. I was looking for drinking water when I happened to come across this blotchy, spotted, and marbled rusting tank. This was not what I first assumed, an intentionally painted abstract work of art; it was just an iron holding tank painted numerous times. An aluminum undercoat had been covered by a succession of black and white paint interspersed with touches of blue and red colouring. I was still not convinced the conceptual effect wasn't deliberate. There were too many semblances to modern art. Even looking closely I could not figure it out and when I asked some locals passing by about the tank they just said it was always a mess.

Pinks and blues

This simple picture tells a story with basically four elements: barn, pasture, sheep and a steep lava hillside. However, if you look closely you will spot three more sheep on the nearly vertical slope. I once stared at a burning candle for about half an hour thinking it was only wax, wick, and flame but ended up with 76 distinct characteristics. Examples are: the wick is about one cm long; the end is black; it is made up of four individual strands; they curl in a right-handed direction; the bottom of the wick is white; the part of the wick closest to the melted wax glows with a reflection of the flame, and so on. Try it not only with a candle but with the images you make. It will improve your photography by forcing you to pay attention to detail that could enhance or diminish an image.

272

If it wasn't for the rattle in the back of my car I would not have stopped here to behold this scene. The riot of colours coming from the Icelandic poppies held me long enough to look about,and take this image. Snow-capped mountain, overhead wires, conifers, property fence, lupins, rocky ditch, white and yellow poppies now all remind me of the time I had to fix a rattle. Photographs are memories you can store.

In the fall this once raging river is reduced to a slow meandering stream and the dust from the well-washed gravel flows with it.

After a short summer, patches of snow still cling to mountainsides and the once bright green moss begins to fade as days shorten and autumn clouds move in.

Shelter

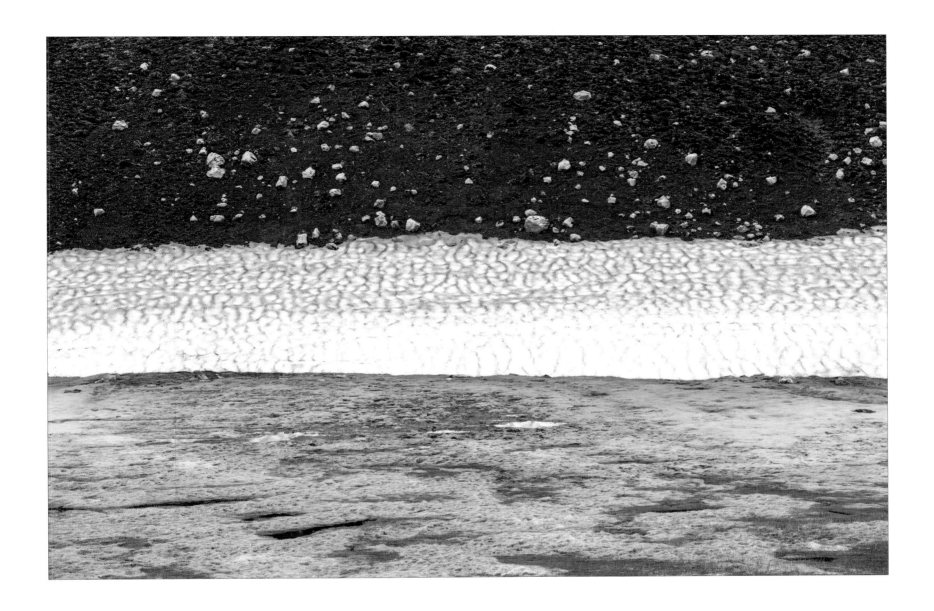

This semi-abstract image of a rocky hillside, band of dirty snow, and a sweep of wet moss illustrates a noteworthy lesson of how the water flow from melting ice is a significant component to generating and sustaining life.

In these infrequent fertile valleys, far from Reykjavik, agriculturalists and their families lead solitary lives on tracts of land that have been passed on for generations.

Appreciated for its flavouring and sweet scent, Angelica Archangelica is used to flavour a variety of home-cooked dishes and is also used as an additive in the production and seasoning of common liquors. Blue lupins have replaced this plant in many of the fields and swamps.

As beautiful as it might be, the lupin plant has become very controversial. Initially introduced to prevent topsoil erosion it has now so dominated some of the countryside as to become a threat to indigenous plant species. The grey woolly moss especially is under threat.

I had found a clearing on the side of a road and under a dark overcast sky close to midnight I pulled over and settled in for another night in the car. Tossing and turning throughout an uncomfortable sleep I rose early to a completely fogged-in landscape. With nothing to see, I stayed behind the wheel, made plans, cleaned my equipment and waited. I was parked facing this stone wall and repeatedly stared up into a curtain of fog totally unaware of what lay behind it. Finally when I sensed a distinct brightening of the sky I again looked up into the mist and was completely surprised. With a fresh morning breeze rising only quick work captured this fleeting moment.

While molten rock rises from a deep magma chamber, breaking through the earth's crust and adding to Iceland's land mass, this ancient shore cracks and crumbles, surrendering to gravity, erosion and the sea. Nature's way of give and take.

I am an opportunistic photographer and do not have a must do list of all the different iconic and well-known attractions of a country. I might visit them but very rarely do I photograph them. I travel by car or wander on foot enjoying exploration. There are no expectations or disappointments, only pleasant surprises. If something attracts me then I analyze it and make a decision whether I want to continue working on the image. I have not calculated my success rate but even after much effort do not press the shutter. Maybe this radical way of operating comes from the days when I used a large format 4 x 5 camera where there was a hefty cost associated with every exposure. I now use a digital camera and there would be no cost associated with taking another image, but once again I learned from experience that the picture would not be improved when I got home and would take up my time considering it once more only to finally dump it.

   This image is a good example of taking advantage of the light and how it can transform a landscape from the mundane to the more imaginative. It reminds me more of sheep grazing in a Scottish landscape under a radiant rainbow than it does of Iceland. No planning here but just being there and pleasantly surprised.

The following images were all taken on the same short stretch of rocky beach but at different times and under a different light. Throughout this day the incoming tide and already powerful waves advanced uninterrupted across the enormous expanse of the cold North Atlantic, gaining in height and strength. It was an ever-changing scene where at one moment it was surprisingly calm and in the next large waves came in groups rising unusually high and quickly crashing onto the shore. Often the ocean displayed this threatening power with large unexpected waves surging forward, rising much higher than the last. Caution is advised here. Many are not aware of the "sneaker" waves, especially prevalent in Iceland, that come in unexpectedly at a greater speed and with a longer unanticipated reach. The unwary person is easily swamped, loses footing in the loose gravel and is carried out to sea. Even though there are signs at the more visited beaches about these dangerous waves, people still have been washed away and drowned. I knew of this possibility and yet there was one time when I was more occupied with my camera settings, unaware of my surroundings, that I had to just grab my tripod and run as well as you can run in ballbearing-like gravel. It was a not-so-gentle reminder that you should never turn your back to the sea.

Dark porous rock, smashing waves, and stormy clouds all combine their rough textures into a wild and dramatic scene.

What a moment it was when I parked the car behind a bluff and heard the thundering of waves smashing on the shoreline. The sea was boiling green and the churning currents raised sediments off the ocean floor into the sepia-coloured foam. It was mesmerizing. Only later, when composing the image, did I notice in the horizon the mounting waves and the distant mountain blurred in mist. The sound has to be imagined.

When I first studied this as a possible image I was attracted to the dry rock firmly nestled against this dripping wall. I was interested in making a composition of the dry and wet shapes and knew It was going to be a complicated image. It is quite common to use a polarizing filter to remove reflections from wet surfaces and deepen the colours beneath. I deliberated the thought but decided against it. Removing the reflections would take away the distinct shape of the rocks and flatten the image. I particularly liked the blue relfections of the sky and just left the image as it was. The clumps of scattered green moss grounded the image and gave it more depth, more of a three-dimensional feel.

290

I have learned that by lingering and being in the moment and not worrying where else you should be your observation skills improve considerably. You come to know and understand the place better, and what at first glance may seem uninspiring can become quite significant. It gives you a greater opportunity to improve a composition and then wait for the right light or, in this case, the right wave to complete the picture. It is, in the long run, more rewarding at the end of the day to know you have put together something of merit. I have witnessed photographers coming up to a scene, quickly snapping an image, crying out, "Wow neat" and immediately turning to leave. I am quite certain their image will not bring back the memory they expect to have.

291

There are many subtle components in this picture and most of them are opposing. A warm yellow light sweeps across the rocky surface of the moraines while in the foreground the light in the shadows remains blue and cool. On one side of the image the landscape is rock-strewn and hard while the other is soft and smooth. The hazy sky is bright with a delicate blush deepening into a subtle pink as it meets the sea, while in the immediate foreground below the steep moraine, the ash is unvaried, solid and dark. Solitary stones, waves, beach and hill now catch my eye.

In this abstract scene the dark elongated sandbars, thin spit of land, and distant islands, all have a harmonious tone and coordinate in unison as one similar component. On the other hand, the grey water and misty sky, also similar in shade, combine to form another tonality. While still maintaining their respective shades and tonalities both blend effectively to shape a minimalistic landscape. In the foreground a single shorebird reflects the vista's dominant hue.

When viewed separately from the rest of the landscape, this highly textured section of coloured tundra at first looks unreal. However, on closer inspection all individual parts ring true. It is a microcosm of green moss that is fresh and new and white moss that is old and dried. The plant life is in all stages of either dormancy, growth or decay. Even the dried roots of the berry plants leave their mark. It is an undulating carpet hundreds of years in the making.

ICELAND

In Iceland this moss is also called the vampire plant because it seems to live forever. Sitting on top of bare rock the plant grows and dies at the same time. While the top is growing the bottom is dying. When conditions are not suitable it loses its colour and hibernates.

This dwarf willow with tightly knitted stems grows close to the ground to retain heat from the earth and avoid the grating wind. The small scattered tufts of grass tell of a coarse impoverished soil depending for replenishment on the grasses' on its own decay.

This exposed hillside, stained with the many tints of blacks, browns, yellows and reds, meets the ash- sprinkled snow at a fringed borderline. At first it appears that the dark shape might be slowly advancing, overpowering the snow, but the movement is really in the receding snow that is giving way to the warming surface. This happens quickly enough that it can be observed if watched closely.

Blue is not my favourite colour, especially in a landscape photograph. In this case, however, I think it is effective, adding to the image as an active colour not necessarily representing the sky but as a blue shape that works in unison with the two other forms of dark and bright.

Our eyes have certain rules of conduct. The one demonstrated here is that we are first drawn to the light where bright shapes move forward and dark shapes recede. Only once the eye has become accustomed to this distinction does our vision resolve to define what is in the darker regions. Once understood, foreground and background combine to reveal the three-dimensional quality of the image.

What attracts me to this image is not only its colour and texture but also how uncertain you are about the sense of scale. Lost in this dilemma the imagination is allowed to flow and I think you would never tire of it. Much of the detail in an image of this size is missing and could only be appreciated in a much larger print.

In a new country with a different environment it is easy to become overwhelmed by the exciting variety of unfamiliar stimuli. It is tempting to take pictures of nearly everything strange. The drawback to this is that most of the images result in just snapshots, the only intent of which is to show that you were there, and this is what it looked like. I have, with experience, learned that to become a more effective photographer I have to slow down and take a picture with a single intent. Shooting here and there never works. It is like chasing two rabbits at the same time. You catch neither. Here I wanted to show how these unusual striations caused by the accumulation of different layers of falling ash run horizontally through a rock wall, and how the lines remain parallel and aligned even in the loosely separating boulders.

In the land of the midnight sun there is a whole new hiking schedule that one can take advantage of. It was very late in the evening when I came upon these magenta coloured hills covered in a rich yellow green moss. The sky was overcast but the sideway rays of the setting sun penetrated enough to paint this unfamiliar landscape in an eery and extraordinary light.

Hard climbing sometimes give you a better point of view.

Iceland is a visual treasure.

Too often we are exposed to images that have a great dynamic range revealing too much detail in the highlights and shadow areas. Sometimes it is good not to see too much and to leave something out, allowing a little bit of mystery to remain.

Sometimes it is best to keep an image simple and let it tell its own story.

This panorama taken in the highlands has much to offer visually. It feels as if I am airborne, looking down onto a green oasis high on a plateau surrounded by fields of snow. In the foreground, snowpacks have rivulets of melt water funneling down ravines, and above mosses thrive in washed-out furrows. Tones of ochres, browns, and greys interspersed with the diverse hues of blue rhyolite rock paint the snow topped hills. Dark blowing dust, accumulating in smaller drifts, adds a painterly effect to the snow and shadowy clouds diffuse an even light.

ICELAND

I think this is a well-balanced image but what puzzles me is where the reddish scree flowing from the enormous rock comes from.

Just as the two sloping hillsides funnel the advancing fog, so also are your eyes funnelled into the bottom of this valley and upwards into the brighter and varied clouds. The vivid foreground, still lit up by a lingering light, draws your eyes back and forth across the valley. Moments later the whole area was squeezed in with the darkening fog and the depth was gone.

ICELAND

This image of ice reminds me of a small incident going through customs on my return trip home. My last eight trips have been either to Iceland or Antarctica and all have been very direct and straight forward in getting there and coming back. For my trips to Antarctica I would arrive at the Ushuaia airport in Argentina, grab a taxi to the dock where my ship was waiting, get on board and settle into my cabin. On my return it is just the same but in reverse. For Iceland I arrive at the airport, pick up my rented car and drive directly into the lava fields. On my return, I drive out of the countryside, drop off the car at the airport and wait for my flight. All so simple. However, sometimes not so when I stand in front of the customs inspection officer trying to explain that my two week sojourn was souvenir-free because I really was not interested and also there was nothing to buy. "Where were you?" was the question. When I mention Antarctica a suspicious eye stares back at me. "What were you doing there?" "Taking pictures," I reply. Now with a little more skepticism she asks. "You really were taking pictures for two whole weeks?" A confident "Yup" from me. Now comes a long examining stare. "Prove it," she says. I pull out my camera from my carry on and open it to a picture of a glacier. Still doubtful, she tries with difficulty to flick through more images so I tell her that she could look at my website. She puts down the camera with a thud and scans her computer. After a long wait she looks back at me. "Do you give lessons?

No matter what rules of composition you assimilate you will never become convincing if you leave out feeling.

ICELAND

The space between these chunks of floating ice is as important as the ice itself.

Remnants of a glacier

ICELAND

Eleven per cent of Iceland is covered in ice. Compared to ninety-six percent coverage in Antarctica, Iceland is obviously a much milder place as a direct influence of the warmer North Atlantic current.

Over this retreating glacier the reflected light scatters brightly through a passing fog

This glacier tongue has over the last year completely disappeared into its own meltwater.

From a glacier a few kilometres away, chunks of ice calve and descend Iceland's shortest river, flow under the bridge, and, with the tide, are deposited on the black lava ash of Diamond Beach.

ICELAND

This image looks as if huge chunks of molten glass were strategically placed over a dark background. It almost looks computer-generated. Having arrived in Iceland the day before and not yet fully attuned to the schedule of the land of the midnight sun, I woke up at 3:30 a.m. thinking it was about 7:00 a.m. Still in my sleeping bag I peeked out of my steamy car window and was pleasantly surprised to see no one on this most popular of tourist attractions. Not to miss this opportunity I prepared my gear as a few tourists were already beginning to arrive. Worried about footprints in the sand I headed to the extreme end of the beach and for a few minutes I was delighted to be alone. Sizes here can be deceiving with the most distant object being waist high.

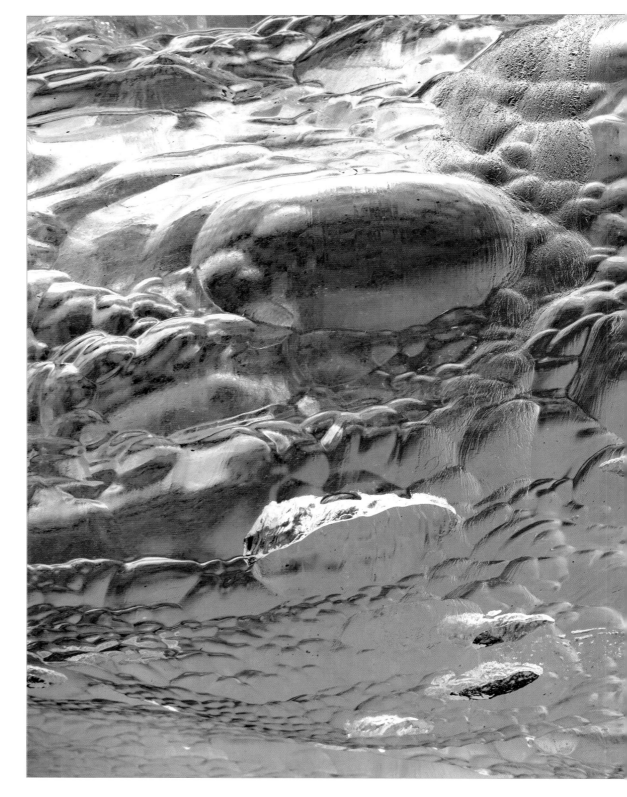

This could easily have been an overlooked image. A careful study makes you wonder what subtle forces shaped these configurations.

ICELAND

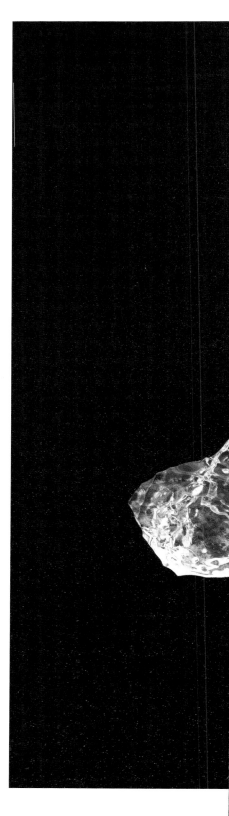

Ice not only comes in an endless variety of shapes but also in clarity, textures, opacity, density, reflectivity, colour, purity, and brightness. Rearranged with each incoming wave it took quick work to move the tripod and compose the image before the next wave followed. Needless to say, all were not successful. This is a colour photograph.

Notes on a music sheet are not all crammed together but have well thought out intervals or rest periods between them. So it is with composing an image that only has a few elements in it. The spaces between them are also studied, measured and chosen. Both in music and in imagery the composition works only if the timing or intervals are well determined. I had no hand in placing these pieces of ice.

Ice not only comes in an endless variety of shapes but also in clarity, textures, opacity, density, reflectivity, colour, purity, and brightness. Rearranged with each incoming wave it took quick work to move the tripod and compose the image before the next wave followed. Needless to say, all were not successful. This is a colour photograph.

Notes on a music sheet are not all crammed together but have well thought out intervals or rest periods between them. So it is with composing an image that only has a few elements in it. The spaces between them are also studied, measured and chosen. Both in music and in imagery the composition works only if the timing or intervals are well determined. I had no hand in placing these pieces of ice.

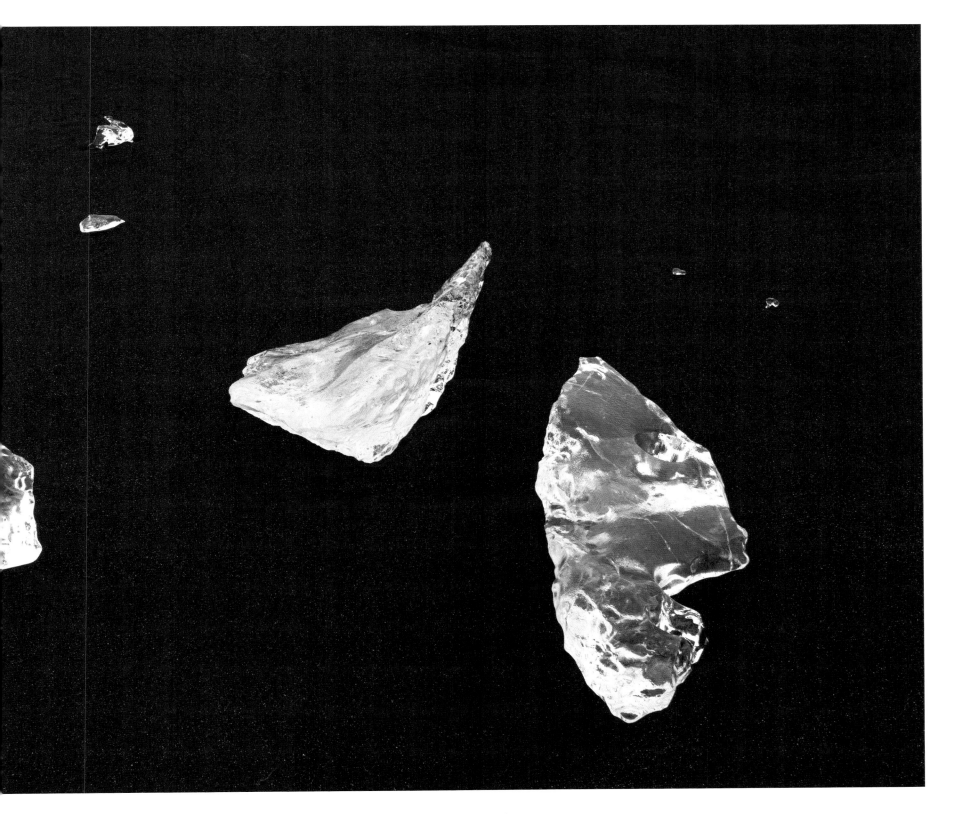

331